YOU ARE SAGARD
You are sailing on the Crimson Sea.

Though the Crimson Sea might be aptly named for the bloodshed that has occurred in it over the centuries, it actually takes its name from the red seaweed that grows in its depth and dyes the water blood-red. Many are the horrifying rumors of monsters believed to dwell in these strange waters.

You are determined that nothing will stop you in your search for the beautiful Ketza Kota, the woman you love. So you have set sail aboard the *Midnight Reaper* with a motley crew of pirates who have no loyalty to anyone. Will you survive . . . or will you become another victim of the terror of the Crimson Sea?

HERO'S CHALLENGE™

SAGARD THE BARBARIAN

GAMEBOOK™

No. 3
THE CRIMSON SEA

by Gary Gygax
and Flint Dille

CORGI BOOKS
A DIVISION OF TRANSWORLD PUBLISHERS LTD

SAGARD THE BARBARIAN: THE CRIMSON SEA
A CORGI BOOK 0 552 52320 8

First published in Great Britain by Corgi Books

PRINTING HISTORY
Corgi edition published 1986

SAGARD and HERO'S CHALLENGE are trademarks of
Gygax/Dille.

Corgi Books are published by Transworld Publishers Ltd.,
61-63 Uxbridge Road, Ealing, London W5 5SA

Printed and bound in Great Britain by
Hunt Barnard Printing Ltd., Aylesbury, Bucks.

THE CRIMSON SEA

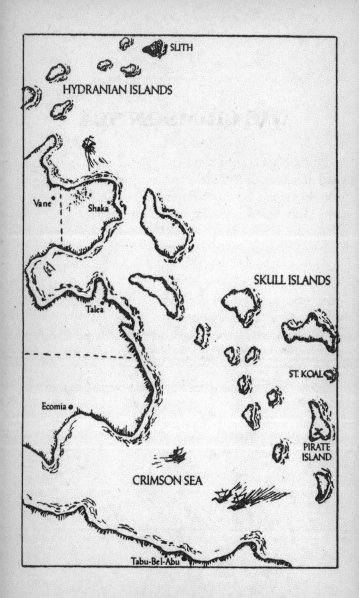

INTRODUCTION

After his adventure on the Isle of Slith, Sagard and his beautiful female companion, Ketza Kota, sought refuge on the pirate island of St. Koal from the Slith Assassins, who lusted for revenge.

As the book begins, Sagard is assumed to be a Level 3 fighter. However, before the book ends, he may well become a Level 4 fighter if he accumulates 60 or more experience marks. Total the points you have received from other books, and add any you receive in this book to the total.

As this story begins, Sagard enjoys the pleasures of a tropical island, but foul winds blow northward from Hitaxia.

Soon the Ratikkan barbarian will experience terror on

The Crimson Sea . . .

SECTION 1

It is said that when the pirates of the realm die, they do not go to the afterworld; instead, they return to St. Koal—the island without law.

Many are the times that you have been forced to defend yourself and Ketza Kota, and many are the ruffians you have triumphed over.

For a time, you have made a home in a cliffside cave overlooking the deep, blue sea. Only a mile away is the island's only city, which is composed of rotting wooden shacks bleached by the burning tropical sun, the ruins of an ancient Vanian fortress, and numerous gaming halls where pirates drink odd concoctions from the shells of coconuts and play games of chance.

On a bright midsummer's day, taking only your sword, you set out with Ketza Kota for Paradise Cove, where a rushing waterfall cascades into the transparent ocean and the reefs abound with conch, lobster, fish, and turtles.

After frolicking in the water for several hours, you lie upon the beach eating mangoes gathered deep in the palm forest and cooled in the transparent water, when suddenly you see a sun-reddened hand out of the corner of your eye. You jump to your feet as a motley figure dashes away carrying your sword.

"Get back here before I make you swallow that sword!" you shout, but the figure keeps running.

Chasing the figure, who appears to be a penniless Freebooter reduced to common thievery, you cross the smooth rocks near the beach and dash up a short path which ends at a precipitous cliff. There, you corner the brigand.

Like a trapped animal, he turns, snarling, and attacks you with an arcing blow. Instinctively, you dive away, and the blade whooshes past you.

After regaining your footing, you grasp several throwing rocks. Your opponent, even though armed with the Valkyrie sword, which will allow him to do 1 extra point of damage each time he hits, is a clumsy lout who has grown soft during his time on the isle. (*Note:* Sagard will be near water through most of this book, so he will have cached his *chainmail shirt* in his cave, if he has gained such a shirt in a previous book.)

As you are unarmed, you must fight one level below your normal level. You have one other option, and that is to grapple with the brigand. In that case, you may not fight but instead flip for a 4. The Freebooter, however, fights after each attempt to grapple. If you successfully grapple the sword away from him, go to Section 9.

If this is your first Sagard book, take a quick look at the combat sheet below and go to the rules in Section 97.

SAGARD (LEVEL 2: 1/0, 2/1, 3/1, 4/2)
[20] [19] [18] [17] [16] [15] [14] [13] [12] [11] [10] [9] [8] [7] [6] [5] [4] [3] [2] [1] (Begin the book again.)

FREEBOOTER (LEVEL 1: 1/0, 2/0, 3/1, 4/1)
[7] [6] [5] [4] [3] [2] [1] (You have defeated your opponent. Go to Section 9.)

If you flee, lose your sword and go to Section 4.

SECTION 2
Bribing the Barmaid

Reaching into the small moneybag at your waist, you show the woman a shiny gold coin. "Ten gold pieces say you can direct me to my friend."

She glances quickly at a table, where four brawny Tehnite gamblers wearing snakeskin garb play cards. One of the Tehnites smiles up at her, and she nervously smiles back.

Leaning forward, she whispers, "Meet me behind the bar. Make sure you are not followed, and be discreet in leaving lest you arouse my swain's jealousy."

Waiting until the Tehnite is absorbed in his card game, you slip out into the balmy night.

Behind the tavern, you find the barmaid waiting and glancing furtively around.

"What do you know of the tattoo?"

"The gold," she says, extending her hand. You give her the ten gold pieces (mark them off your *status chart*), and before she speaks she inspects each coin in the misty light.

"The tattoo belongs to men who have crewed on the ships of Salamar Rabfahd, as scurvy a seadog as you will find. You will find his ship, the *Midnight*

Reaper, anchored just off shore. Now, go quickly—before my beau sees that I am gone."

As you turn to leave, a voice bellows out behind you. "I'll teach you to stay away from my wench, Ratikkan dog!"

Turning, you see the enormous Tehnite lumbering toward you, a wide and deadly broadsword in one hand and a short finishing dagger in the other.

As he draws closer, you have a choice. You can either engage him in combat (go to Section 10), or you can try to escape him (go to Section 14).

SECTION 3
Defeating the Slaver

The Slaver stumbles backward and collapses into the red-tinged surf. Before you can chase the Slavers' craft further, you see the gray dorsal fins of great white sharks streaking toward you.

You instinctively flee to shallow water as hungry sharks devour the man who had once called himself the Barracuda.

Gain 2 *experience marks* and head to Section 7.

SECTION 4
Fleeing the Freebooter

As the Freebooter raises his sword to finish you off, you summon your last strength and somersault off the cliffside.

Your fall seems to take hours as you descend toward dark rocks that jut out of the roiling surf. Just as it seems that your short life has come to an end, luck intervenes, and you land in a patch of water between the jutting rocks.

Bubbles float around your head, and small, brightly colored fish dart for cover. In seconds, you rise to the surface again and swim for Paradise Cove.

Nearing the cove, you see a small, gray-masted sloop sail away. Shrill screams meet your ears, and you see Ketza Kota, her wrists bound, sailing away. You realize that the theft was only a diversion to separate you from Ketza Kota and that she has fallen into the hands of Slavers.

Even your most powerful strokes will not carry you to the boat quickly enough, and you swim desperately for shore. Go to Section 7.

SECTION 5
Fleeing the Slaver

The Slaver very nearly impales you with a quick jab.

Ducking, you lose your balance and fall into the waist-deep water. The Slaver, laughing with the thrill of victory, closes in for the kill, unaware of the triangular shark fins speeding up behind him.

Instinctively, you turn and flee as murderous sharks devour the man who had once called himself the Barracuda.

Reaching the shore, you watch helplessly as the Slavers' mast shrinks in the distance. Go to Section 7.

SECTION 6
The Gaming Halls

"I haven't seen any tattoo like that before in my life!" the barmaid, dressed in a lacy blouse and leather skirt, says as you show her a rough drawing you made of the tattoo on the arm of the dead Slaver.

Sensing that a few gold pieces might oil her tongue, you consider bribing her. If you have ten gold pieces from previous books, they might gain you valuable information. (Subtract the gold from your *status chart* and go to Section 2.) If you don't have the gold, or if you do have it and want to save it, keep reading.

Waiting a few moments for a bribe, she finally turns away and speaks to a man at the end of the bar. Their conversation, in low voices, seems to concern you, for you frequently see them glancing at you and snickering.

As you empty a tankard (regain *3 hit points*), you observe the crowd in the club. Tall, thin-faced Chandanese criminals play complex games of strategy while smoking long pipes and discussing philosophy. Leather-vested Yatians and Drakosians adjust the daggers in their wrist sheaths while carefully watching their cards, and loud Hitaxians laugh and dribble wine down their chins onto their gold-bedecked chests while they roll ornate dice.

Suddenly, you see something that pours fire into your blood. At the door stands the Freebooter who stole your sword. As your eyes meet, you leap into action.

The Freebooter turns and dashes out of the inn.

Giving chase, you knock into a table and have to dodge a drinking glass thrown by an angry Vanian.

On the street, you hear the fleeing footsteps of the Freebooter. "Stop! Or this time I shall cut you to ribbons!" you shout.

He keeps running. You chase him through maze-like streets and finally corner him in a dark alley piled high with refuse.

"Tell me where the woman is, and I will spare you," you say, drawing your sword.

"Rot you, Ratikkan!" he shouts back.

SECTION 7
Reaching the Shore

Standing on the beach, you grimly watch the Slaver boat disappear on the horizon. You grit your teeth. "I will rescue you, Ketza Kota!"

Ketza Kota was not taken easily. A Slaver lies dead on the sand, the hilt of Ketza Kota's poniard protruding from one of his eyes. He looks like any other pirate on St. Koal: his skin is olive colored, his clothes are gaudy, he wears a ring through his hooked nose, and his scimitar is clutched in one hand. However, one shoulder is painted with a distinctive tattoo of an enormous creature crushing a galleon in one hand.

If you did not get your sword back, take his *cutlass*. It will allow you to fight at your normal combat level. Taking a seat on the shore, you rest from your ordeal and try to figure out what to do. Regain 8 *hit points*.

Slavers cruise the waters of the Skull Islands like wolves in search of fattened sheep. Their origins range from the Vulzar Kingdom to the extreme north to Tukotan in the distant south. While nobody is safe from these merchants of flesh, they most often abduct able-bodied men and beautiful women.

Reasoning that Ketza Kota was taken for her beauty, you can only assume that she is destined for the harem of a Hitaxian sultoon, or for a kingdom farther north where captured women—especially beautiful ones—are forced into unholy servitude.

There are two places where you may search for the beautiful Slith woman. You can either try to learn the identity of her dead would-be captor in the gaming halls of St. Koal (Section 6) or head to the slave markets on the chance that she was taken there (Section 13).

SECTION 8
The Freebooter Talks

The Freebooter lies on the ground, begging, "Spare me, and I shall tell you all that you want to know." (Gain *1 experience mark*.)

"Where do I find the woman you helped to capture today?" you ask, holding the cold steel of your sword to his throat.

"I know nothing," he says, eyes filled with terror.

"You lie!" you respond, jabbing with your sword.

"They will torture me if I tell you anything . . ."

"I'll do worse than that if you don't."

"They were Slavers from the *Midnight Reaper*. It is anchored just off shore."

"You had best be telling me the truth, Freebooter. And you had best stay out of my sight, or I shall cut you to ribbons."

He nods fearfully and slowly crawls away. For a moment, you consider setting him free from his miserable existence, but cutting down an unarmed man is repugnant to you, so you spare him.

Armed with this information, set out for the *Midnight Reaper* in Section 16.

SECTION 9
Defeating the Freebooter

The Freebooter swings wildly, misses you, and stumbles off balance. Seizing your chance, you jump him and pry your sword from his hand. (Regain your *sword* and gain *1 experience mark*.)

As you regain the sword, the frightened brigand runs to the cliffside and jumps off. Scrambling to your feet, you watch him hit the water and disappear below the surface in a high geyser.

Moments later, he surfaces again, shouting to you. "We have your woman, Ratikkan fool!"

Looking down on the beach, you see that a small, dark-sailed ship has landed on the shore and three Freebooters are wrestling with Ketza Kota. Heart pounding, you dash back down the cliffside. As you run, you realize that the Freebooters are in fact Slavers, and the attempt to steal your sword was a ruse to separate you from Ketza Kota.

You reach the cove as the Slavers shove her onto the ship and sail away. Blood rushing through your veins, you dash after it.

As you run toward the craft, one of the Slavers, dressed in gaudy silk, brandishes a cutlass and jumps into the shallow water after you. "I, Brahmat the Barracuda, shall add one Ratikkan to my score of kills."

As you approach, he swings the cutlass at you, misses, and sends a spray of water into the air.

As the Slaver stands between you and the boat, you must fight him.

SAGARD (LEVEL 3: 1/1, 2/1, 3/2, 4/3)
[20] [19] [18] [17] [16] [15] [14] [13] [12] [11] [10] [9] [8] [7] [6] [5] [4] [3] [2] [1] (Begin the book again.)

SLAVER (LEVEL 3: 1/1, 2/1, 3/2, 4/3)
[14] [13] [12] [11] [10] [9] [8] [7] [6] [5] [4] [3] [2] [1] (You have defeated your opponent. Go to Section 3.)

If you flee, go to Section 5.

SECTION 10
Fighting the Tehnite

Drawing your sword, you face off against the Tehnite. The barmaid, more terrified by the Tehnite than you are, shouts to him, "Thank heaven you are here to save me from this barbaric Ratikkan!"

You turn and look at her in stunned surprise. "What are you talking about?" you ask her.

She whispers to you. "Beat the scum and I am yours."

Utterly confused, you look back and forth between the Tehnite and the barmaid. The Tehnite suddenly lets out a deep, bellowing war cry and charges. He strikes first.

SAGARD (LEVEL 3: 1/1, 2/1, 3/2, 4/3)
[20] [19] [18] [17] [16] [15] [14] [13] [12] [11] [10] [9] [8] [7] [6] [5] [4] [3] [2] [1] (**Begin the book again.**)

TEHNITE SWORDSMAN (LEVEL 3: 1/2, 2/3, 3/3, 4/4)
[24] [23] [22] [21] [20] [19] [18] [17] [16] [15] [14] [13] [12] [11] [10] [9] [8] [7] [6] [5] [4] [3] [2] [1] (**When you have defeated your opponent, go to Section 12.**)

Flee to Section 14.

SECTION 11
Over the Wall

His companion defeated, the second Tanzulan guard jabs viciously at you with his spear. Wielding your sword, you hack the spear in half. The guard looks at you in stunned amazement, then flees down the battlements. (Gain *3 experience marks*.)

A throng of shackled slaves in the courtyard below cheers. More Tanzulan guards, stationed at towers on the opposite side of the battlements, run toward you.

Taking advantage of the chaos, you grab a set of keys from a prostrate guard and throw them to the slaves, who begin releasing themselves.

As the guards near you, you jump from the wall to the courtyard. A clanging bell sounds, and more guards swarm into the courtyard. Freed slaves, using their chains as weapons, fight their captors.

Using your sword as an axe, you smash open the shackles of many slaves as a battle breaks out. If this is your first group battle of the Sagard series, read the rules carefully, because battles involve both group and individual combat.

BATTLE FOR FREEDOM

You are about to engage in a multiple-force battle. The battle is fought in consecutive rounds between the slaves and the guards.

First, count the number of guards, and flip for each one. The guards kill slaves with a flip of 3 or 4. (Cross out one slave for each 3 or 4.)

Next, count the number of slaves left, and flip for each surviving slave. Slaves kill guards with flips of 4 only.

Before each round of combat, Sagard has the option of individually fighting one guard per round. Each time Sagard defeats a guard, deduct one from the force. In individual combat, guards are Level 2 fighters with 11 hit points.

GROUP COMBAT

SAGARD'S SLAVES (1/0, 2/0, 3/0, 4/Kill)
[29] [28] [27] [26] [25] [24] [23] [22] [21] [20] [19]
[18] [17] [16] [15] [14] [13] [12] [11] [10] [9] [8] [7] [6]
[5] [4] [3] [2] [1]

GUARDS' FORCE (1/0, 2/0, 3/Kill, 4/Kill)
[12] [11] [10] [9] [8] [7] [6] [5] [4] [3] [2] [1]

INDIVIDUAL COMBAT

SAGARD (LEVEL 3: 1/1, 2/1, 3/2, 4/3)
[20] [19] [18] [17] [16] [15] [14] [13] [12] [11] [10] [9]
[8] [7] [6] [5] [4] [3] [2] [1] (**Begin the book again.**)

GUARDS (LEVEL 2: 1/0, 2/1, 3/1, 4/2)
  Guard #1 [11] [10] [9] [8] [7] [6] [5] [4] [3] [2] [1]
  Guard #2 [11] [10] [9] [8] [7] [6] [5] [4] [3] [2] [1]
  Guard #3 [11] [10] [9] [8] [7] [6] [5] [4] [3] [2] [1]
  Guard #4 [11] [10] [9] [8] [7] [6] [5] [4] [3] [2] [1]

If you defeat all of the guards and have ten men left, gain *3 experience marks* and go to Section 18.

If you defeat all of the guards but do not have ten men left, gain *2 experience marks* and go to Section 6. Knowing that Ketza Kota is not in the slave pens, head off to the "pirate" gaming halls.

You may *not* flee.

SECTION 12
The Barmaid's Pleasure

Having given the Tehnite swordsman a good throttling, you turn to the barmaid. She smiles. "Oh, thank you, brave Ratikkan, for you have saved my life."

Knowing that you have just participated in the barmaid's favorite recreation, have taken hit points to boot, and, for that matter, have proved little, you slink off into the night.

Go to Section 16.

SECTION 13
Moonlight on the Battlements

Long ago, the great Vanian king, Garagus Rex, conquered the Skull and Hydranian islands and thus ruled over an empire that extended from Hitaxia on the south to the Vang-Ko River on the east and the Aerdy to the north.

The reign of Garagus Rex was long and brutal, but his great kingdom soon collapsed. Upon his death, his seven sons struggled for rule. The outcome of their fratricidal wars was the Garagian Federation, seven small states allied in war and in bitter rivalry in peace.

Throughout the islands are broken remnants of Garagus's rule. One of them is St. Koal Castle. Its gray battlements look out over the ocean like a brooding despot. Long out of service, the old castle was converted into a slave market, and the great walls, which were once built to keep invaders out, now hold people in.

Late at night, after resting for the afternoon (gain 7 *hit points*), you climb a tall cliff that leads to the Vanian castle. Peering up, you see tall, thin Tanzulan guards carrying long spears silhouetted against the high towers.

Throwing a cloth-wrapped grappling hook to the top of the thirty-foot wall, you begin your ascent. As you climb, your feet slip on the crumbling walls and send a shower of small pebbles clattering to the ground.

You wait motionlessly in the shadows, praying under your breath that the great god Telchur will dim the guards' senses. Fortune smiles on you as you hear the guards chatter among themselves.

"The slaves . . . they smell and attract rats . . ."

"But we are slaves," another says.

"We are different. We hold spears."

With a devilish smile, go to Section 17.

SECTION 14
Fleeing the Tehnite Swordsman

Trying to get yourself out of a stupid fight, you take flight into the satiny night. The Tehnite swordsman follows for a while, but his leather armor slows him down, and in no time you have left him and his foul curses behind you.

Gain *2 experience marks* for having the good sense to get out of this fight before you were killed, and go to your destination at Section 16.

SECTION 15
Over the Wall

Knowing that you are about to be impaled by the Tanzulan guards, you jump off the parapet. Whizzing through the night sky, you see only the churning water below. Desperately, you try to veer closer to the castle, but the seaward winds bouncing off of the walls blow you out.

At the last second, you jab your sword into the soft rock cliffside, and it sticks. You hang for a moment, your heart pounding, and then swing yourself back up to the ledge.

The two Tanzulan guards throw their spears. Flip, and take 5 hit points for each 4 you get.

Dragging yourself back to the cave you and Ketza Kota lived in, you rub salve on your wounds and rest for a day. Regain *15 hit points* and set out for the gaming halls, where you may learn the identity of the Slavers.

Go to Section 6.

SECTION 16
The *Midnight Reaper*

A warm tropical moon glows through a layer of lacy mist and onto the purple sail of the *Midnight Reaper*, which is anchored just off shore. The ship is of beautiful design for slaving and pirating. A large cog, she is propelled mainly by a single large sail but has oar slots for windless seas. Mounted at the back of the ship is a fighting tower for combat, and another fighting platform is mounted on the prow.

Spotting a small rowboat near you, you contemplate two possible strategies. You could sneak aboard the ship and look for Ketza Kota (Section 36).

Or you could boldly row up to the ship and declare that you wish to join her crew, in order to gain their trust and access to the ship (Section 23).

SECTION 17
Assault on the Slavers

Slowly, you climb up the wall and mount the parapet. Below you is a throng of slaves from nearly every region in the realm: fair-eyed Aerdians, well-muscled Tehnites, white-haired and red-eyed Vulzars, and dark Tanzulans, Wugas, and Zymbians.

You take the guards totally by surprise; therefore, you get three swings before they can respond.

SAGARD (LEVEL 3: 1/1, 2/1, 3/2, 4/3)
[20] [19] [18] [17] [16] [15] [14] [13] [12] [11] [10] [9] [8] [7] [6] [5] [4] [3] [2] [1] **(You have been defeated. Go to Section 19.)**

TANZULAN GUARD #1 (LEVEL 2: 1/0, 2/1, 3/1, 4/2)
[14] [13] [12] [11] [10] [9] [8] [7] [6] [5] [4] [3] [2] [1]

TANZULAN GUARD #2 (LEVEL 2: 1/0, 2/1, 3/1, 4/2)
[11] [10] [9] [8] [7] [6] [5] [4] [3] [2] [1]

When you have defeated your opponents, go to Section 11.

If you flee, it means you are jumping off the well, hoping to land on a narrow cliffside ledge. Go to Section 15.

SECTION 18
Assault on the *Midnight Reaper*

Tanzulan guards flee in all directions. Hitaxian slavers, who less than an hour ago looked regal in their lavish gowns bedecked with jewels, now beg for mercy at the hands of slaves.

Running through the crowd, you search in vain for Ketza Kota. She is neither among the living nor the dead. Coming upon a young woman about Ketza Kota's age, you beg her for information about the girl.

"No girl like that has yet come in here, but I know that the Sultoon Jazeer has placed an order for several young women."

"Placed an order with whom?" you ask.

"The Slaver, Salamar Rabfahd."

"And where is he?"

"He has a boat. It is known as the *Midnight Reaper*," she says.

Turning to the anxious crowd, you shout in your loudest voice, "You have your freedom!"

They cheer with a bubbling frenzy as you continue speaking. "Now I intend to help you keep it. Let us take control of the *Midnight Reaper* and sail far away from here!"

A thundering roar of approval greets you. Leading the crowd, you charge through the streets of St. Koal and off to the docks. The thrill of victory and the aid of a Wuga witch doctor heal your wounds. (Gain *16 hit points*.)

Reaching the docks, the teeming crowd searches for the *Midnight Reaper*. Finally, a toothless Gyptic shouts to you, "Thar she be!"

Just off shore, a warm summer moon shines

through a layer of tropical mist and onto the *Midnight Reaper*. The ship is of beautiful design for slaving and pirating. A large cog, she is propelled mainly by a single large sail but has oar slots for windless seas. Mounted at the back of the ship is a fighting tower for combat, and another fighting platform is mounted on the prow.

Seeing the galleon, you motion to the crowd to swim to the ship and board it. The next few moments are a flurry of activity. All of the surviving slaves swim with the heightened energy of newly begotten freedom.

A pirate guarding the ship lets out a call of alarm, but before he can raise his cutlass a captured Tanzulan spear pierces him in the chest. Freed slaves board the ship like a swarm of ants, some shinnying up the ropes and letting down rope ladders to the others.

As you board, an enormous man steps onto the deck. His robes are of an ornate silk, and his turban blazes with the light of a blinding jewel. He scowls at you from behind a curved mustache as he pulls a two-handed cutlass from a wide sash.

"If you are to take my ship, you must kill Salamar Rabfahd first," he says in a husky voice tainted with a Hitaxian accent.

"Gladly," you say, pulling your sword. "But before you die, tell me where I can find Ketza Kota."

"I know of no such creature," he responds.

"Your men kidnapped her this afternoon."

"Ah . . . A beautiful wench she was. She'll be in the hands of the Sultoon Jazeer shortly."

"Then I shall have to make quick work of you!" you say, moving in on the massive pirate.

In moments you are locked in deadly combat. He will be a tough opponent, but if you take him the *Midnight Reaper* will be yours. You strike first.

SAGARD (LEVEL 3: 1/1, 2/1, 3/2, 4/3)
[20] [19] [18] [17] [16] [15] [14] [13] [12] [11] [10] [9]
[8] [7] [6] [5] [4] [3] [2] [1] **(Begin the book again.)**

RABFAHD (LEVEL 4: 1/1, 2/2, 3/3, 4/3)
[18] [17] [16] [15] [14] [13] [12] [11] [10] [9] [8] [7] [6]
[5] [4] [3] [2] [1] **(You have defeated your opponent. Go to Section 20.)**

You may *not* flee Salamar Rabfahd.

SECTION 19
Defeated by the Tanzulas

The last thing you see is the flash of a Tanzulan spear, and then darkness descends on you. For days you fade in and out of a murky twilight. Faces appear and disappear in front of you. Some of them are the kindly faces of other slaves; others are the hard, cruel faces of guards. You lose your *sword* and *treasure*.

In a vague haze, you see a familiar hook-nosed face peering down on you. It is the Freebooter you fought on the cliff. "I know that man," he mutters. "I fought him while the others captured his woman for the Sultoon Jazeer. A pretty harem girl she will make."

Even in your stupor, your hackles rise. You try to grab the man, but your arms, still weak, fail to reach him.

Days pass, and gradually you come to realize that you are in the slaving pens. As your strength grows, you test the steel chains that hold you, but they are much too strong.

Finally, when your strength has grown sufficiently (regain *all hit points*), your new masters put you up on the market blocks, where buyers bid on you. In the first afternoon, a massive Hitaxian privateer employed to discourage sea trade, wearing a turban and elaborate robes with a long cutlass at his sash, steps up to you.

"I will take him. He will make a good galley slave."

As the pirate and the Slaver haggle over a price, fire burns in your chest, but you conceal it because your only hope for freedom is to escape from the Slavers.

Thus begins your life of slavery. Go to Section 30.

SECTION 20
The Cutlass

Mortally wounded, Salamar Rabfahd crashes to the deck, shaking the timbers of the ship. There is a moment of silence as you bend down and take his cutlass.

Rabfahd's *cutlass* is a powerful *weapon*. Any time you use it you gain 2 *extra hit points* per swing. Therefore, if you would normally do 1 hit point of damage, you will now do 3 hit points. However, the cutlass will always miss (do no damage) when you flip a 4.

Wiping it off, you hear fleeing footsteps and see several other Slavers run onto the deck and dive over the side of the ship.

Letting out a loud guffaw, you call to your crew, "Let us sail south, for I have a score to settle with the Sultoon Jazeer!" (Gain 4 *experience marks* for your victory.)

Assembling a crew of experienced slaves, you set sail into the velvety night. For two days you sail southward toward the Crimson Sea. (Regain *all hit points*.)

Go to Section 28.

3

SECTION 21
Treasure on the Isle of Dread

Upon hearing this story, the pirates eye you suspiciously before a lanky young sailor steps forward. "I have heard tales of treasure on the Isle of Dread."

"But why should we believe you know where it is?" another pirate asks.

As the pirates step toward you, you respond, "Why would I lie to you? You will cut me to shreds if we reach that island and there is no treasure."

For a tense moment, the sailors mutter to each other. Sweat breaks out on your brow.

Then, spontaneously, they charge up to the captain's cabin. You hear loud growls and thuds as the captain fights his fate. As strong as he is, he cannot defeat so many men. He is dragged from his hammock to the side of the ship and dumped over along with his first mate.

You reach the deck as the gigantic captain hits the water, letting out a string of curses. "I will have revenge, Sagard. I will have revenge!" As the voice dies away, a chill goes up your spine.

Note that your crew is composed of pirates and go to Section 28.

SECTION 22
Fleeing the Gnarled Pirate

The Gnarled Pirate takes a vicious swipe at you with his cutlass and jars your sword from your hand. Sensing certain death, you turn to flee but don't get far before you feel a sharp crack on the back of your head. You black out as you tumble to the deck.

When you awake, you discover that heavy chains bind your limbs. When your vision clears, you discover that you are chained to the slave galley along with several other sweaty prisoners.

For days you sit in the steamy galley while the ship is at dock. Now and then, surly pirates bring you cups of obscene-tasting stew, and slowly you regain *all of your hit points*. Lose your *sword* and go to Section 30.

SECTION 23
Joining Rabfahd's Crew

Paddling the rowboat to Rabfahd's ship, you let out a bellowing call. "Let me aboard!"

In moments, three husky pirates peer down at

you. "What business do you have aboard the *Midnight Reaper?*"

"I wish to join the crew, and you would be well advised to take me!"

The three men laugh loudly and toss down a rope ladder. As you climb the rope ladder, they shake it wildly in an attempt to throw you off, but nevertheless you reach the deck.

The captain of the ship, a giant, looks down on you with ill-concealed scorn. "You want to join my crew, do you? Then you'll have to fight for the chance." He motions to one of his crewmen, a tall Fexian dressed in crimson with a mouth of rotted teeth and gold.

Flip to see who strikes first. Even means you strike first; odd means the Gnarled Fexian Pirate strikes first.

SAGARD (LEVEL 3: 1/1, 2/1, 3/2, 4/3)
[20] [19] [18] [17] [16] [15] [14] [13] [12] [11] [10] [9]
[8] [7] [6] [5] [4] [3] [2] [1] (Begin the book again.)

FEXIAN PIRATE (LEVEL 2: 1/0, 2/1, 3/1, 4/2)
[16] [15] [14] [13] [12] [11] [10] [9] [8] [7] [6] [5] [4]
[3] [2] [1] (When you have defeated your opponent, go to Section 24.)

Flee to Section 22.

SECTION 24
Beating the Fexian Pirate

The Fexian Pirate is sprawled on the deck. (Gain *1 experience mark*.)

Rabfahd peers at you with mixed suspicion and admiration. "Rarely have I seen a man fight with such deadly efficiency," the pirate captain says. "I could use a fighter like you on my ship."

One of his mates steps past you, picks up the Fexian Pirate's carcass, removes his shiny gold teeth, and throws the lifeless body over the side. "And you'll need another crewman."

"I'll join," you say, "if the pay is good and the food is better."

The Hitaxian pirate lets out a bellowing laugh. "You will join on my terms. For your other choice is instant death."

Go to Section 25.

SECTION 25
Sagard the Pirate

A brisk ocean breeze catches the skull-emblazoned sail of the *Midnight Reaper*, and the great craft is carried out to sea. For the first several days, you watch closely as the sailors go about their business. You quickly learn the skill, thus concealing your inexperience at sea. (Regain *all hit points*.)

Late one night, as the pirates sleep, you inspect the ship. There are no slaves to be found except for the galley crew. Approaching the first mate, you ask where the slaves have gone, and you are told that they were sent on to Tabu-Bel-Abu, the main seaport of Hitaxia. Somehow, you must get there.

Fortunately, fate intervenes to help you. Keeping your ear peeled for the scuttlebutt, you hear rumblings of discontent among the crew. It seems that Salamar Rabfahd has been cheating his men.

One morning, a Medigian freighter is spotted. It is a slow, lumbering craft, and the men are anxious to pirate her. However, Rabfahd declares that the craft is not to be attacked.

Bitter rumors spread among the crew like wildfire. Some say that Rabfahd has turned coward, while others say he has struck an agreement with the Medigians and that they are paying the pirate not to attack their ships.

As the sun goes down, you sense that the moment is ripe for mutiny. Calling several crewmen together, you prepare your speech. The right speech can provoke a mutiny. One wrong word and they will turn against you.

As the pirates secretly gather, three modes of persuasion have crossed your mind. You consider appealing to their greed and telling them of a mythical land of treasure in the Crimson Sea. You could appeal to their anger with the captain, claiming that you will give them a fair share of the booty. Or you could simply tell them the truth about Ketza Kota and hope that out of sympathy they will join your quest.

All of the approaches are risky, and yet all of them have their merits. As the throng of fractious pirates gathers before you, you must pick one of the three following speeches:

1. "Hear me, mates! I have it on good information that Captain Rabfahd has not only cheated us on our booty, but he has also gone behind our backs to accept money from certain countries to spare their ships. We can take no more of this treachery! I say we grab the captain while he sleeps and throw him overboard!" (If you want this option, go to Section 27.)

2. "I must tell all of you the truth about why I have become a mate on this ship. Days ago, a dear friend of mine was kidnapped by slavers and taken in one of Rabfahd's boats to Hitaxia. I have come aboard to get her back. I will put an end to Salamar Rabfahd's reign of terror. Join me, men, and we shall clean the Hitaxian scum from the sea." (If you want this option, go to Section 38.)

3. "I have it on good information that there is treasure to be found on the Isle of Dread. A hoard of treasure greater than the imaginings of any man! And should we find that treasure we shall all be rich and retire to luxury forever. Let us throw this scoundrel Rabfahd from his ship and get on with our hunt." (Go to Section 21.)

SECTION 26
Carcass Overboard

The Gnarled Pirate is stretched across several stolen casks of wine. (Gain 2 *experience marks*.)

Turning, you prepare to depart the ship when you come face to face with the enormous Hitaxian pirate and two of his mates.

"Rarely have I seen a man fight with such grace and power," the pirate says. "I could use a good fighter like you."

One of his mates steps past you, picks up the lifeless Gnarled Pirate, and throws his carcass over the side. "And we'll need another crewman."

"I'll join your crew," you say, "if the pay is good and the food is better."

Salamar Rabfahd lets out a bellowing laugh. "You will join on my terms. For your other choice is instant death."

Go to Section 25.

SECTION 27
Toppling the Unfair Master

"And how do we know that you will be better?" one of the men shouts.

"You have my word!" you respond.

"The word of a pirate is nothing," he shouts back.

Insults bounce back and forth on the deck like stray sparks in a tinderbox, and in moments a lively fight breaks out in the hold between those who support you and those who are against you. Fists crack into jaws, elbows thump into stomachs, and loud curses fill the air.

Suddenly, the massive figure of Salamar Rabfahd fills the doorway, and his bellowing voice quells the melee. "Silence!"

Looking you in the eye and drawing his mighty cutlass, Rabfahd calls to you, "Let us settle this as men! You and I, lad, shall duel to the death. To the winner goes the ship."

You must fight Rabfahd. Flip to determine who goes first. Even means you strike first; odd means he strikes first.

SAGARD (LEVEL 3: 1/1, 2/1, 3/2, 4/3)
[20] [19] [18] [17] [16] [15] [14] [13] [12] [11] [10] [9] [8] [7] [6] [5] [4] [3] [2] [1] (**Begin the book again.**)

SALAMAR RABFAHD (LEVEL 4: 1/1, 2/2, 3/3, 4/3)
[23] [22] [21] [20] [19] [18] [17] [16] [15] [14] [13] [12] [11] [10] [9] [8] [7] [6] [5] [4] [3] [2] [1] (**When you have defeated Rabfahd, go to Section 29.**)

Death awaits you if you attempt to flee.

SECTION 28
Adventure on the Crimson Sea

Though the Crimson Sea might be aptly named for the bloodshed that has occurred in it over the centuries, it actually takes its name from the red seaweed that grows in its shallower depths and dyes the water blood-red in parts. Many are the horrifying rumors of monsters believed to dwell in this ocean.

At this point, make sure you have noted the constituency of your crew, for your voyage will take on very different aspects depending on who your crew is.

If your crew is composed of slaves, mark that on the Sagard *status chart* and go to Section 37.

If the crew is composed of pirates who have mutinied, note that on the Sagard *status chart* and go to Section 32.

SECTION 29
The Death-Dealing Blow

Salamar Rabfahd, covered in his own blood, stares at you. A hideous light grows in his eyes, and his stength seems to return. Raising his two-handed cutlass, he prepares to strike at you, but before he delivers a death-dealing blow his body goes rigid and he crashes to the deck.

The crew members, even those who had vilified you earlier, cheer. (Gain *4 experience marks* and regain all your *hit points*.)

Placing one foot atop the captain's lifeless body, you proclaim yourself captain. "Now, men, we shall strike at the heart of Hitaxian shipping and make ourselves wealthy. We shall sail to the Crimson Sea!"

Before throwing the pirate captain's body overboard, you take his mighty cutlass.

Rabfahd's *cutlass* is a powerful weapon. Any time you use it you gain 2 *extra hit points* per swing. Therefore, if you would normally do 1 hit point of damage, you will now do 3 hit points. However, the cutlass will always *miss* (do no damage) when you flip a 4.

4

Note on your *status chart* that your crew is composed of pirates and go to Section 28.

SECTION 30
Sagard the Galley Slave

For days, the soft clanking of your leg-irons rattles in your ears. You were not made to be a slave, and you find the task disgusting. You plot jumping the first mate, who holds the keys to your shackles.

Each night, when the others have fallen asleep, you work the rusty bolt that fastens your chain to the ship. For the first several days, it stubbornly resists your efforts, but finally the bolt snaps and you can break loose whenever you want. Now you must find the right time.

An old, gnarled Fexian deckhand is on watch. As he steps back and forth, his cutlass dangling from his belt, you contemplate jumping him. If you want to do so, go to Section 33. If not, continue reading, but remember that you cannot turn back.

A day passes, and you carefully observe the movements of the crewmen. On the following evening, the first mate, a swaggering fellow, cruises down the row and whips the men. "Work harder, you lazy cuss!"

As he comes to you, he looks at you with a particularly nasty grin. "Now, Ratikkan dog, will you row or must I whip you harder?" His lash strikes your back, and you recoil in pain. Anger swells in your heart.

At dawn the following morning, Salamar Rabfahd steps down to inspect the ship. "Today we must sail far; thus, I demand that you work to your limits. Any man lagging behind will be cast to the sea!"

As he passes you, his eyes light up. "This man's shackles have come undone. Seize him immediately."

Springing up, you attack the captain. Your first move is to attempt to pull the cutlass from his side. Go to Section 44.

SECTION 31
On Treacherous Reefs

Through the night, winds and currents throw the *Midnight Reaper* around like a leaf in the wind. Even your most experienced sailors are seasick.

Many times in the crashing surf you see the hull narrowly miss enormous rocks, but on the following morning the sun rises in the east and the seas are calm.

Return to the map in Section 39 and aim your ship away from shore.

SECTION 32
A Voyage for Plunder and Treasure

Take a quick glance at the map in Section 39. Since the mutiny against Rabfahd, the scurvy pirates have viewed you with great suspicion, muttering mutinous words under their breath.

Also, you are plagued with talk of buried treasure on the Isle of Dread.

Therefore, if you wish to avoid mutiny, you must do two things: explore the Isle of Dread before going to Hitaxia *and* attack every Hitaxian galleon that you come upon.

Go to the map in Section 39.

SECTION 33
Fighting the Guard

As the old pirate nears you, you grab him before he can go for his cutlass. With the element of surprise as your ally, you slam him in the face, and the two of you begin fighting. As you are not armed, you fight at one level below your normal combat level. You strike first.

SAGARD (LEVEL 2: 1/0, 2/1, 3/1, 4/2)
[20] [19] [18] [17] [16] [15] [14] [13] [12] [11] [10] [9] [8] [7] [6] [5] [4] [3] [2] [1] (Begin the book again.)

GUARD (LEVEL 1: 1/0, 2/0, 3/1, 4/1)
[10] [9] [8] [7] [6] [5] [4] [3] [2] [1] (You have defeated the Guard. Go to Section 41.)

You may *not* flee.

SECTION 34
Battling the Pirates

As the pirates thunder down the stairs, you set the galley slaves free. This will be a multiple-combat battle, so read the rules carefully if you haven't done this before.

You are about to engage in a multiple-force battle. The battle is fought in consecutive rounds between the galley slaves and the pirates.

First, count the number of pirates and flip for each one. The pirates kill slaves with a flip of 3 or 4.

Next, flip for each surviving slave. Slaves, casting off the yokes of their past masters, kill pirates with flips of 3 or 4.

Before each round of combat, Sagard has the option of individually fighting one pirate per round. Each time Sagard defeats a pirate, gain *1 experience mark* and deduct one member from the force. In individual combat, pirates are Level 2 fighters with 13 hit points.

GROUP COMBAT

PIRATES' FORCE (1/0, 2/0, 3/Kill, 4/Kill)
[18] [17] [16] [15] [14] [13] [12] [11] [10] [9] [8] [7] [6]
[5] [4] [3] [2] [1]

SARGARD'S SLAVES (1/0, 2/0, 3/Kill, 4/Kill)
[31] [30] [29] [28] [27] [26] [25] [24] [23] [22] [21]
[20] [19] [18] [17] [16] [15] [14] [13] [12] [11] [10] [9]
[8] [7] [6] [5] [4] [3] [2] [1]

INDIVIDUAL COMBAT

SAGARD (LEVEL 3: 1/1, 2/1, 3/2, 4/3)
[20] [19] [18] [17] [16] [15] [14] [13] [12] [11] [10] [9]
[8] [7] [6] [5] [4] [3] [2] [1] (Begin the book again.)

PIRATES (LEVEL 2: 1/0, 2/1, 3/1, 4/2)
   PIRATE #1 [13] [12] [11] [10] [9] [8] [7] [6] [5] [4]
[3] [2] [1]
   PIRATE #2 [13] [12] [11] [10] [9] [8] [7] [6] [5] [4]
[3] [2] [1]
   PIRATE #3 [13] [12] [11] [10] [9] [8] [7] [6] [5] [4]
[3] [2] [1]

If you defeat all of the pirates, regain all your *hit
points*, mark the crew type as slaves on the Sagard
status chart and go to Section 28.

You may *not* flee.

SECTION 35
Defeating Salamar Rabfahd

Salamar Rabfahd crashes to the deck of the ship. (Gain 3 *experience marks* and regain all your damage points.)

Not wasting an instant, you cut the other galley slaves free. Arming themselves with their chains, they scream through the ship, beating the pirates as they sleep. Though you shout at the top of your lungs for them to stop the brutal fighting, they carry out their carnage until not a single pirate survives.

Reaching the deck, they cry in unison for you to be their captain. Raising your sword, you vow to sail into the Crimson Sea, where you will find them a home. Mark the crew type as slaves on your Sagard *status chart*.

You have Rabfahd's cutlass. It is a powerful weapon. Any time you use it you gain 2 *extra hit points* per swing. Therefore, if you would normally do 1 hit point of damage, you will now do 3 hit points. If you flip a 4, however, you have missed and therefore do no damage to your opponent.

Go to Section 28.

SECTION 36
Sneaking Aboard the
Midnight Reaper

Paddling up to the fighting ship, you hear the loud, rhythmic snores of the watchman from high up on the crow's nest. Making as little noise as possible, you make your way to the anchor chain, which holds the enormous craft to the bay.

The ship is dark except for a flickering light in the captain's quarters. Peering through a small window to his cabin, you see a massive Hitaxian playing cards with a scruffy lot of men.

Creeping past the cabin, you step below deck to the galley, where slave oarsmen sleep chained to their seats.

You cross quietly through the crew's bunking area, where a pair of drunken pirates snore loudly. Taking a stair downward, you find yourself in the hold. The gentle lapping of waves and creaking of the ship's timbers are the only sounds. Ketza Kota is not aboard the *Midnight Reaper*.

Suddenly, there is a flash of light, and an oil lamp begins to burn. In the dim light you see a gnarled Fexian pirate with a long gash down his face and a black hole where an eye once was.

"And what might you be doing aboard this ship, laddy?" he asks.

Before you can respond, he answers his own question. "Trespassing aboard Salamar Rabfahd's vessel can only get you one thing: dead!" With that, he charges you with his cutlass. Flip to see who strikes first. Even means you strike first; odd means he strikes first.

SAGARD (LEVEL 3: 1/1, 2/1, 3/2, 4/3)
[20] [19] [18] [17] [16] [15] [14] [13] [12] [11] [10] [9] [8] [7] [6] [5] [4] [3] [2] [1] **(Begin the book again.)**

GNARLED PIRATE (LEVEL 3: 1/1, 2/1, 3/2, 4/3)
[17] [16] [15] [14] [13] [12] [11] [10] [9] [8] [7] [6] [5] [4] [3] [2] [1] **(When you have defeated your opponent, go to Section 26.)**

Flee to Section 22.

SECTION 38
For the Maiden Ketza Kota

Finishing an emotion-filled speech on the loss of Ketza Kota, you await the crew's response. It is not long in coming. As one, the crew erupts in a volley of spontaneous laughter. The laughter quickly turns mean, and they converge upon you with menacing intent. You try to draw your sword, but after a heroic struggle they wrest it from your grasp and raise you high into the air.

Squirm and beg as you might, you cannot escape the muscular pirates as they carry you to the deck and toss you into the murky sea.

As the *Midnight Reaper* vanishes into the night, you look around for a nearby island to swim to. There is none. By morning you shall be food for the fishes.

Begin this book again.

SECTION 39
The Crimson Sea

Before reading this section, turn to the map of the Crimson Sea. Then come back.

Sailing on the Crimson Sea is very simple. In order to sail, draw an arrow from the hex you are in (shown as the starting point on map) pointing to the hex you want to go to. Because of the tricky winds and currents of the sea, your ship may be blown off course. The winds and currents are simulated by flipping the pages before moving.

After drawing the arrow to the hex you want to go to, flip the pages. If you flip a 2 or a 3, you go to that hex. If you flip a 1, you go to the hex counterclockwise (to the left) of the hex you are aiming at. If you flip a 4, you go to the hex clockwise (to the right) of the one you are aiming at. This may cause you to enter the same hex more than once.

Arriving in the new hex, pick the hex you want to go to, flip again, and repeat the process. Keep repeating the process until you land on a lettered hex, and go to the section indicated on the legend. In that section, you may run into combat, and the rules for those battles will be explained there.

At no time may you leave the map or point your ship in a direction that might take you off the map. Also, you may not sail onto land. If your flip takes you onto a land hex, you are shipwrecked. You may only land safely in a port. Once in port, you may either venture onto the land, repair your ship, or both.

You may not go to port on the same island twice.

Bearing in mind that the Crimson Sea is filled with hostile Hitaxians, treacherous jutting rocks, and vicious creatures, sail very carefully. Turn to the map for your voyage on the Crimson Sea.

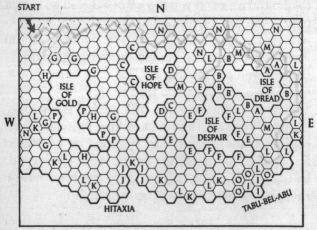

1

Legend

A	Section 80	I	Section 95
B	Section 51	J	Section 45
C	Section 54	K	Section 50
D	Section 55	L	Section 71
E	Section 43	M	Section 52
F	Section 59	N	Section 93
G	Section 40	O	Section 69
H	Section 84	P	Section 46

If your ship runs into a hex containing land, go to the *shipwreck* section for that land:

Shipwreck on the Isle of Gold: Section 48
Shipwreck on the Isle of Hope: Section 57
Shipwreck on the Isle of Dread: Section 51
Shipwreck on the Isle of Despair: Section 61
Shipwreck on Hitaxian shore: Section 53

If your ship is *sunk*, go to Section 66.

Ship Hit Points
_____
_____
_____
_____

SECTION 40
The Phantom Mist

Your senses tingle as the *Midnight Reaper* passes through a misty fog which seems to hover over the ocean like a curtain of death. Anything could hide in the mist, which brings with it a deathly silence.

You must flip the pages each time you go through a hex of mist. If you flip a 1, go to section 93; if you flip a 2, go to Section 52; if you flip a 3, go to Section 71; and if you flip a 4, go to Section 42.

SECTION 41
Flying Fists

A roundhouse blow knocks the Guard flat on his back, and he tumbles across the deck. (Gain *1 experience mark*.)

The sounds of your fight have awakened not only

the galley slaves but also the pirates above, and you hear rushing footsteps.

Flip the pages. If you get a 1 or a 2, keep reading. If you get a 3 or a 4, go to Section 34.

Before you can release any of your comrades, two pirates charge into the galley. Because you now have a cutlass, you may fight them at full strength. You strike first.

SAGARD (LEVEL 3: 1/1, 2/1, 3/2, 4/3)
[20] [19] [18] [17] [16] [15] [14] [13] [12] [11] [10] [9]
[8] [7] [6] [5] [4] [3] [2] [1] **(Begin the book again.)**

PIRATE #1 (LEVEL 2: 1/0, 2/1, 3/1, 4/2)
[9] [8] [7] [6] [5] [4] [3] [2] [1]

PIRATE #2 (LEVEL 2: 1/0, 2/1, 3/1, 4/2)
[6] [5] [4] [3] [2] [1]

If you defeat your opponents, gain *1 experience mark* and go to Section 34.

You may *not* flee.

SECTION 42
Fearful Voyage Through the Mist

The *Midnight Reaper* drifts slowly through the mist. The men aboard your ship, though tough as nails, grasp tightly the strange religious items that hang from their sunburned necks as the curtain of fog drifts past.

Strange sounds of drowned screams catch your ears, but there are no assaults on your ship.

Conscious of the horror you are heading into, return to the map in Section 39 and flip again. You have made it through one hex of the mysterious mist.

Go back to the map and keep sailing.

SECTION 43
Ghost Currents

A stiff current, like a giant's hand, pushes the *Midnight Reaper* toward the shallow reefs off the Isle of Despair, where you see vaguely human shapes running in and out of the jagged palm trees lining the coast.

Though you cannot see them clearly, a tinge of fear creeps up your spine, made worse by the grim assessment of an old salt who stands beside you.

"Even the Hitaxians shun this blasted island. They say it's a graveyard for demons."

Flip the pages. If you flip a 1 or a 2, go to Section 61. If you flip a 3 or a 4, go to Section 31.

SECTION 44
Fight with the Captain

Jumping from your seat, you knock the captain backward. As he tries to regain his balance, you pull his enormous two-handed cutlass from his sash.

Rabfahd's *cutlass* is a powerful *weapon*. Any time you use it you gain 2 *extra hit points* per swing. Therefore, if you would normally do 1 hit point of damage, you will now do 3 hit points. However, the cutlass will always *miss* (do no damage) when you flip a 4.

As you prepare to do battle with Rabfahd, he demands a cutlass from one of his men and gets it. You strike first.

SAGARD (LEVEL 3: 1/1, 2/1, 3/2, 4/3)
[20] [19] [18] [17] [16] [15] [14] [13] [12] [11] [10] [9] [8] [7] [6] [5] [4] [3] [2] [1] **(Begin the book again.)**

SALAMAR RABFAHD (LEVEL 4: 1/1, 2/2, 3/3, 4/3)
[22] [21] [20] [19] [18] [17] [16] [15] [14] [13] [12] [11] [10] [9] [8] [7] [6] [5] [4] [3] [2] [1] **(When you defeat Rabfahd, go to Section 35.)**

You may *not* flee Salamar Rabfahd.

SECTION 45
The Hitaxian Fort

After battling a fierce wind and drifting slightly off course, the pilot tries to right the ship's direction. Suddenly, the man in the crow's nest shouts a cry of alarm as a sizzling ball of fire passes over the ship and splashes into the water next to you. Wheeling around, you see the jagged battlements of a Hitaxian fortress on a distant cliff.

You must get away from the fort before the Hitaxians turn the *Midnight Reaper* into firewood. In order to do so, you must flip a 4. The Hitaxians, meanwhile, fire on you. Combat against Hitaxian catapults works like land combat. At each turn, you flip to flee the fort and then, if you were not successful, the Hitaxians fire at your vessel.

HITAXIAN CATAPULT FIRE (1/0, 2/0, 3/1, 4/4)
(When you have escaped, mark any damage given to the ship and go back to the map in Section 39 and sail away from the Hitaxian fort.)

MIDNIGHT REAPER
[30] [29] [28] [27] [26] [25] [24] [23] [22] [21] [20]
[19] [18] [17] [16] [15] [14] [13] [12] [11] [10] [9] [8]
[7] [6] [5] [4] [3] [2] [1]

SECTION 46
Port on the Isle of Gold

The setting sun casts an orange glow on the white sand beaches and lazily tilted palm trees of the Isle of Gold. Dropping anchor, you stare out at the island, wondering why no settlements have been built on a place so beautiful. Gain 2 *experience marks* for successfully bringing the ship into a port.

A wizened old sailor, his face lined by the beating sun and stinging winds of the sea, mutters to himself. "A place could only be so beautiful for one reason: to conceal a great evil."

If you want to make repairs on the *Midnight Reaper*, do so now. Flip the pages, multiply the number you get by 4, and restore that number of hit points to your ship.

After making repairs, you may either set sail (go back to the map in Section 39) or grant your men shore leave on the island (go to Section 49).

SECTION 47
High Tide

Panicked, you and your surviving men flee through the island. The tropical plants, which were beautiful in the fading sunlight, have turned to razor-sharp cutting leaves in the moonlight, and everywhere you see hideous crawling crustaceans crashing through the thick undergrowth in pursuit.

Paddling as quickly as you can, you and your men make it to the craft as the grotesque creatures crawl into the water.

In fevered haste and with a smaller crew, you prepare to sail. As grasping claws probe the side of the ship, you float off the sandbar and into the moonlit sea.

A few tough whacks of your sword cut the last clawing demon off the ship. Your adventure on the Isle of Gold is behind you. (Gain *1 experience mark*.)

You would be well advised to make haste for port on the Isle of Hope, where it is rumored that there are available sailors.

Return to the map in Section 39 and begin sailing from where you left off.

SECTION 48
Phantom Reefs

Relying on memory, the old navigator aboard the *Midnight Reaper* winds through the treacherous reefs of the Isle of Gold. For several hours, the voyage goes well despite the fact that you seem to be cutting very close to a perimeter of sharp crags which protrude from the ocean like tombstones.

Without warning, you hear a loud screech from the bottom of the ship, and everybody is thrown forward. You have run aground. (Lose 2 *ship strength points*.)

Knowing that the ship will be able to sail again once high tide comes, you have a choice. You may either head ashore and investigate this intriguing island, or you may wait in your ship until high tide. If you want to go ashore, go to Section 49. To keep sailing, point the ship away from shore and keep going.

SECTION 49
Shadows in the Moonlight

You tingle as you step onto the Isle of Gold. You could not put the feeling into words, but there is something unnatural about this island. It is too beautiful.

As the sun sets in the west and stars begin to show, your men build a bonfire and cook dinner rations. It is good to set foot on land again, for, though you have adapted to the ocean, you are by nature a man of the woods. As you swallow a drink made of island fruit, you discern strange, furtive movements among the palms.

Someone, or something, is watching you. Taking your sword, you slip away from camp to find out what is stalking about.

Lit by the icy moonlight, the white sand seems to glow. Hearing footsteps in the sand, you conceal yourself behind a spiked tropical bush. Your heart pounds like a Hukka drum. A shadowy human figure passes by. As the figure draws close, you leap out with your sword.

Holding cold steel to the figure's back, you ask, "Who are you?"

The figure turns. It is a beautiful woman. Long dark hair falls from her head in a cascade of curls, and her white skin glows like a lacy cloud in the sky. She is dressed for the jungle, wearing only a short dress of silky native fabric and flowers in her hair.

Embarrassed, you lower your sword. "I'm sorry if I scared you," you say.

She giggles and motions for you to follow her.

"I have to return to my friends," you say. Realizing that she doesn't understand your language, you signal her to follow you back to the camp. To your surprise, she follows, giggling.

Reaching camp, you are startled to discover your men dancing with several other young women who look and are dressed like the girl with you.

Your senses tingle as you watch the dancing.

Something is wrong.

"Relax, Sagard," a sailor calls to you. "This is a night for festivity."

One of the women, who appears to be the leader, motions to the others. The dancers join hands. For a few moments, exotic women and sailors dance hand in hand in a circle. The circle soon becomes a line, and they all dance down a moonlit path.

The tropical woman smiles a broad, innocent smile, takes your hand, and bids you to join the dancing line. Feeling awkward, you go with her.

The dance takes you and your men far inland, down a valley, and finally to the bamboo gates of a small compound. Passing into the compound, you discover that these strange creatures do not live in houses, or even grass huts, but in enormous shells!

Each shell is nearly twice the height of a human and half as wide as it is tall. Outside the hut are small gardens of exotic flowers.

In the center of the bizarre compound is a small amphitheater. Taking a seat, you watch as festivities begin. The tribeswomen play foreign-looking musical instruments made of shells which produce hypnotic, gentle melodies.

Suddenly, you are struck with a horrifying realization. There are no men in this tribe! As no species can survive without members of both sexes, a disturbing question comes to mind.

Where are the men?

Sinister thoughts cross your mind. The men may be robbing your ship while the women dance. They may be out hunting and will be very unhappy upon their return. Or, worst of all, they may all be dead!

Maybe you are just taking things too seriously. The women look innocent, and they have made no aggressive or threatening moves, yet somehow your barbarian instincts scream in warning.

When the song ends, you quickly stand up and address the crowd: "Men of the *Midnight Reaper*. As we must sail at dawn and the night grows short, we must bid our hostesses good night."

Your orders are met with grumbles, but your men comply. Suddenly, a hideous transformation begins. Feminine hands turn into hideous claws, smiling mouths turn into biting jaws, and soft figures turn into hideous-looking, crablike creatures.

Instinctively, you jump away as a massive claw menaces you.

"Run!" you shout. Your men, confronted with the ghoulish beasts, flee. Though the mollusk creatures are deadly, a running man is faster.

As you run, the screams of your shipmates sting your ears as they are torn apart in the jaws of these shape-shifting demons.

Flip the pages twenty times and deduct 1 ship strength point for each 4. Mark this on your ship strength chart. If you have run out of ship strength points, begin the book again. Otherwise, go to Section 47.

keep their dark-mailed armies from invading. While their neighbors to the north struggle in the fields, the Hitaxians demand a percentage of the revenues to buy off invasion and keep trade routes running. Scarcely anywhere in the realm is there a coin that is not stained with Hitaxian sweat, and almost nowhere in the realm is there a slave who has not at one time or another been whipped on the Hitaxian trading docks.

Thus, when the billowing sails and fat hulls of a Hitaxian ship sail over the horizon, you look forward to revenge. You do not have to plunder the ship. If you want to do so, go to Section 74. If not, return to the map in Section 39.

SECTION 51
Run Aground

The coast of the Isle of Dread is littered with the remains of ships that have failed to make the crossing. As you pass close to its shores, your crew eyes the skeletons of dead ships warily, but the helmsman expresses confidence that sailing in this placid sea will be easy.

Suddenly, the ship is struck by a stiff wind. The helmsman fights frantically for control of the ship, but it seems nothing can stop the sharp drift into the island.

Men dive for cover as a loud screech echoes from deep in the hull. Timbers snap as they are dashed against rocks, and suddenly everybody is thrown forward. You have run aground. (Lose *4 ship strength points*.)

After inspecting the damage, you set out to make repairs, leaving several crew members behind to pump water from the hull.

Not far down the shoreline, you find a beached Hitaxian galleon and decide to explore its abandoned cabins.

The great ship is strangely eerie inside. It does not seem to have been smashed by the waves. The food supplies are fully stocked. The longboats are missing. And, strangest of all, it has not been looted. In the captain's cabin, you find a chest of gold coins. Your share is *400 gold coins* (note this on your *status chart*).

Clearly, the men who once sailed this ship had not met their ends at the bottom of the ocean. They had walked off the boat—but to where?

Taking wood from the galleon, the crewmen quickly make repairs on the *Midnight Reaper*. Repair 3–12 ship points by flipping the pages three times. Taking foodstuffs from the abandoned Hitaxian galleon, you and your crew set out to prepare supper on shore and wait for the high tide to take you back to sea. Return to the map and keep sailing.

SECTION 52
Batmosian Marauders

In the western seas lies the Isle of Batmos. Many are the stories of its beauty, and many the tales of the serenity and peace that pervade the island. Men of the sea, Batmosians have learned to ride fish the way men of the land have learned to ride horses. Legend has it that a Batmosian fishing procession is one of the most beautiful sights in the realm.

However, even among the best of people, there are those who are evil. When a Batmosian son or daughter shows signs of a dark nature, he or she is banished to the sea. Because of this policy, colonies of banished marauders have sprung up near trading routes throughout the realm.

Without warning, your ship is struck by a flock of arrows. Spinning around, you see a most disturbing sight. Strange creatures, half human and half scaled, ride enormous fish which they steer by the whiskers, firing long harpoon arrows at the *Midnight Reaper* with deadly accuracy.

These are Batmosian marauders. Fighting them works like land combat, except that you use ship strength points and you do not inflict damage points on the Batmosians. You either kill them or you

.don't. Therefore, when you have one kill, cross off a Batmosian. When you have two kills, cross off two, and so on.

They shoot first.

MIDNIGHT REAPER (1/Kill 1, 2/Kill 1, 3/Kill 2, 4/Kill 3)

[30] [29] [28] [27] [26] [25] [24] [23] [22] [21] [20] [19] [18] [17] [16] [15] [14] [13] [12] [11] [10] [9] [8] [7] [6] [5] [4] [3] [2] [1]

BATMOSIANS (1/0, 2/0, 3/2, 4/5)
BATMOSIAN #1
BATMOSIAN #2
BATMOSIAN #3
BATMOSIAN #4
BATMOSIAN #5

When you defeat the Batmosians, gain *2 experience marks* and return to the map in Section 39.

The *Midnight Reaper* may *not* flee these swift creatures.

SECTION 53
The Black Current

Since the beginning of time, the eastern shore of Hitaxia has been protected from foreign invasion by the Black Current. This strange current, not found anywhere else in the world, runs about the shores of Hitaxia like a rushing river, thus preventing any kind of a landing.

For this reason, when the *Midnight Reaper* drifts too close to the shore, it is thrown from the shoreline by the current. Go back to the map in Section 39 and move one space along the shore toward Tabu-Bel-Abu.

SECTION 54
The Churning Ocean

As you approach the Isle of Hope, the skies turn dark and cloudy. Fearing the worst, you order the helmsman to take you out to sea, but it's too late! Lightning slashes the sky, and the roar of thunder shakes the ship. A torrent of rain floods the deck, and men are washed overboard to meet their deaths in the churning ocean. (Lose *4 ship strength points*.)

As night draws near and mountainous waves rip across the deck of the *Midnight Reaper*, you and your crew fight for your lives. One wrong move and you will be dashed upon the shore of the Isle of Hope.

Flip the pages. If the number is even, go to Section 31. If the number is odd, go to Section 57.

SECTION 55
A Fair Wind

A soft tropical wind blows back your hair as you drift toward the Isle of Hope. (Gain 2 *experience marks* for successfully landing the ship.)

"She's a beauty, ain't she?" a sailor next to you mutters, pointing to the gentle beach which curls around the island like a sleeping cat.

"That she is," you respond. "It is strange that nobody lives here."

At this point you may do repairs on the *Midnight Reaper* if you need them. To determine how many ship strength points you regain, flip the pages and multiply the number you get by 5. After repairing the ship, you may either sail away (go back to the map, Section 39) or you may explore the Isle of Hope (Section 56).

SECTION 56
Trek Through the Isle of Hope

Because islands are separated from the mainland by vast stretches of water, many species of plants and animals survive on them that would be eliminated by predators on the mainland. For that reason, you are not surprised to find species of birds and plants on the Isle of Hope that you have never seen before.

Bananas nearly the size of men grow in profusion on the island, along with fully developed six-inch-tall oak trees. For hours you wander under the hot sun, watching brightly colored birds hopping from branch to branch and numerous other friendly animals splashing around in cool ponds.

Near the center of the island, you spy a high waterfall which reminds you sadly of the waterfall near Paradise Cove where Ketza Kota was kidnapped, and you feel a pang in your heart.

Massive oval boulders protrude high above the waving palm branches. Wanting to gain an aerial view of the island, you step across a sandy palm grove to climb one of the great boulders.

Much to your surprise, you discover that steps have been chiseled out of the huge monolith by human hands. One hand on your sword, you climb upward until you come upon a cave crudely chiseled out of the rock.

As there is no sign of human habitation near the cave, you step inside to investigate. It is dark and damp. The walls are emblazoned with beautifully painted hieroglyphics and ghoulish paintings of reptilian monsters ripping palms out of the ground with gnarled claws. A chill comes over you, and you start to back out of the haunting structure.

Suddenly, you feel a sharp pain in your back. A voice speaking a language unlike any you have ever heard whispers in your ear. Not knowing what to do, you let a hand pull the sword from your sash. Raising your hands, you slowly turn around.

Behind you, holding crude stone weapons, stand seven young women. They wear only grass skirts and blouses of intricately woven flowers which accent their exotic beauty. Looks of wonderment twist their faces as they anxiously speak to each other, admiring your sword.

For several moments they seem to be locked in fervent debate over who you are. Several times they try to speak to you in a soft, lilting tongue, and several times you try to tell them that you do not speak their language. Finally, one of them begins beating on a painting of a dragon with her sword and speaking to you in an impassioned tone.

Deciding that these women are not nearly as dangerous as you might have thought, you take your sword back and sheath it to show you have no intention of harming them.

For several minutes they try to speak to you, but you do not understand a word and attempt to explain, in both words and gestures.

"Ah, you are a Ratikkan," one of them finally says in a voice so free of accent that, were it not for her exotic appearance, you would think she was a Ratikkan. "We have been trying to determine what tongue you speak."

"You speak Ratikkan?" you say, unable to conceal your surprise at her flawless speech.

"We speak virtually every known tongue in the world—and several dialects of each. Once this island was an academy, but now—the Sardonus has destroyed everything."

"The Sardonus?" you ask.

"Oh, you don't know. We had hoped you and your men had come to destroy him."

"Maybe we will, but first we must know what he is," you answer, still intrigued by the curious creatures.

2

One of the women points to a painting on the wall. "That is him when he is awake. For now, he sleeps."

Leading you to the door of the cave, the woman points across the tops of the palm trees to a mountain not far away. "There he is," she says.

"It is a mountain," you say. "Not a dragon."

They nod warily. "It is a dragon."

You are barely able to contain your laughter, but as it would be rude to laugh at these lovely creatures, you hold it in. "I will take you there and show you that it is just a mountain."

The women look back and forth at each other and speak amongst themselves in a lilting language. As pleasant as it is to listen to, you can tell they are involved in some kind of bitter argument. Finally, their leader speaks. "I will come with you. The others are afraid."

You set out for the mountain with the young woman, who identifies herself to you as Mowanna.

"Why don't you women send your husbands to the Sardonus?" you ask.

"I have no husband. The Sardonus ate all of the men."

Squinting your eyes, you can imagine how superstitious people could delude themselves into thinking the mountain was a sleeping dragon. Its general shape is that of a large lizard in repose, and its rocky sides, devoid of foliage, look like reptile skin.

As you reach the base of the mountain, you spy a river that leads into a gaping cave inside the mountain. Mowanna whispers to you, "The Sardonus is drinking."

"That is a mountain cave, Mowanna, not a mouth."

She cowers behind a rock, peering at the cave. Knowing that even the most outlandish superstitions are based on a grain of truth, you wonder what secret this mountain might hold, for obviously somebody has gone to the trouble of creating a myth around it. Perhaps it might even house a great store of treasure.

"Just to prove it, I'll go into the cave," you say, and boldly step into a shallow stream and trudge toward the cave. For just a flickering of a second, it looks to you as if the mouth of the cave has moved!

Steeling your courage, you step toward the cave. It is unlike anything you have ever seen before. Water flows rapidly through columns of stalactites and stalagmites which look like the teeth of a mighty beast.

Once again you consider turning back, but as you look back at Mowanna you see that she has been joined by a number of your shipmates.

"Go ahead, Sagard. We're with you all the way!"

one of them shouts jokingly. Not wishing to be branded a coward by your shipmates, you carry on with the trek even though it has become decidedly distasteful.

Once you pass through the jawlike entrance, all is dark. The only sounds you hear are a soft gurgling and a rush of wind from deep inside the cave. As you step further, you are startled as the wind blows back in from outside—like breathing.

A cold chill rips up your back as you step on something squishy. Suddenly, the ground below you pulls away.

In the flash of an instant, the stalactites and stalagmites move up and down, and you realize that they are indeed teeth. A forked serpentine tongue flicks back at you and slaps you against the cave walls which, instead of being stone, are soft and mushy like flesh. Drawing your sword, you hack at the tongue as the enormous teeth drop down toward you.

The jaws open once again, and you hear a deep roar from the beast's belly. Feverishly, you try to run back out of the jaws, but they close, leaving you in the pitch darkness of the beast's mouth. Suddenly, everything shakes, and you hear the awful grinding of the beast's teeth. One wrong step and you will be pulverized.

Knowing that there is no way out, you have to fight the only way you can—by attacking through the throat of the beast. This will be hard, however, for the great muscles of its throat expand and contract, and torrents of wind rush from inside it as it tries to spit you out.

As you reach the back of the throat, the great mouth opens again, and you realize that the beast has stood up. Looking out through the teeth, you see your shipmates far below, firing spears and arrows at the beast.

Terrified by the hideous roars and torrents of wind from deep inside the monster, you climb down the throat. Muscles contract, nearly crushing you, and you jab your sword into the walls to keep from being sucked into the stomach, which will be filled with hideous acids that will dissolve you in seconds.

There is no way out. The only way you can kill this beast is to survive long enough to cut your way to its heart.

You must fight the Sardonus. At the same time, your men will fight him from the outside. Therefore, you must keep two battles going simultaneously. The battle works like this:

1. Sardonus flips against Sagard. The Sardonus has 50 hit points. For each turn, you will flip for him. If he flips anything but a 4, you are all right. If he flips a 4, then flip again. If he flips another 4, you are swallowed. Take 8 damage points per round until you or the Sardonus is dead.

2. After he has flipped, you flip, fight at your normal level, and mark off the damage you have done against him.

SAGARD (LEVEL 3: 1/1, 2/1, 3/2, 4/3)
[20] [19] [18] [17] [16] [15] [14] [13] [12] [11] [10] [9]
[8] [7] [6] [5] [4] [3] [2] [1] (**Begin the book again.**)

SARDONUS
[50] [49] [48] [47] [46] [45] [44] [43] [42] [41] [40]
[39] [38] [37] [36] [35] [34] [33] [32] [31] [30] [29]
[28] [27] [26] [25] [24] [23] [22] [21] [20] [19] [18]
[17] [16] [15] [14] [13] [12] [11] [10] [9] [8] [7] [6] [5]
[4] [3] [2] [1]

3. Sardonus's attack against Sagard's crewmen. Sagard has ten crewmen. You will flip for each of their turns. The Sardonus kills one crewman with a 3 and 3 crewmen with a 4; flips of 1 or 2 are misses.

SAGARD'S SURVIVING CREWMEN (LEVEL 2: 1/0, 2/1, 3/1, 4/2)
[10] [9] [8] [7] [6] [5] [4] [3] [2] [1]

4. Flip for each of Sagard's surviving crewmen. They fight at Level 2.

When you have defeated your opponent, go to Section 58.

You may *not* flee. If Sagard is killed, begin the book again.

SECTION 57
Shipwreck!

As the night wears on, the storm racking your ship turns into a full-blown hurricane, and the crashing of thunder merges with the sound of your hull slamming into the water.

Suddenly, a loud crack reverberates throughout the ship. Peering into the hold, you see that the hull has been split in two on the sharp head of a boulder. Water floods into the ship, and crew members who had been manning the pump are swept into the murky darkness.

As you head down the ladder to save them, another sharp crack reverberates through the ship. The *Midnight Reaper* is in trouble.

Flip the pages and lose 5 *ship strength points* for each number you flip. (For example, if you flip a 2, lose 10 ship strength points.)

If you have run out of ship strength points, go to Section 66. If you have ship strength points remaining, turn about and keep sailing (Section 39 map).

SECTION 58
A Terrifying Roar

With all your strength, you drive your sword into the monster's vitals. The Sardonus lets out a terrifying roar and crashes to the ground. As you crawl out of the mouth, tremors from the fall shake the island, cracking the surface like glass in jagged patterns around the dying form. (Gain 5 *experience marks*.)

Not pausing to tempt fate, you run as far from the beast as you can. For hours the massive beast twitches and shakes its legs and its tail, uprooting palms with every flick.

As the monster dies, crowds of people emerge from their hiding places and cheer you, bedecking you with flowers and showering you with gifts. The other crewmen who did not take part in the battle join you.

By nightfall, a great feast has been prepared in your honor. Natives dance, exotic foods simmer in massive cauldrons, and songs are sung about you and your men.

If your men are pirates, go to Section 62; if your men are slaves, go to Section 60.

SECTION 59
The Slave Market

The Isle of Despair teems with life. The harbor, which stretches from end to end in a nearly perfect half-circle, is lined with small, brightly colored buildings of wood, stone, and thatch. Small outriggers paddled by muscular islanders, black-sailed Fexian scows and jagged, mysterious Chandanese junks drift in and out of the port like wooden ghosts.

Dropping anchor in the gentle bay, you set the men to making repairs on the ship. Flip the pages and multiply the number you get by 2. Gain that many *ship strength points*. If you want more ship strength points, you may set off to the island with all of your *gold pieces*. If you do not have any gold pieces, set sail. To hire additional sailors, keep reading. If you do not need more ship strength points, go back to the map in Section 39.

The village teems with life. Island women sell bananas, oranges, and other fruits to the strange strains of music played on weird instruments. Broken men hang around dingy taverns, beggars pull on your sleeve for coins, and street vendors hawk their wares.

In a square behind the shorefront buildings is a trader's market where experienced sailors sell their skills to the highest bidder. When you arrive, there are two other traders in the market: a shifty-eyed Hitaxian and a crude Medigian. Flip the pages. If you get an even number, keep reading. If you get an odd number, go to Section 63.

As you reach the market, there are only fifteen men hiring out their services. For each man you hire, gain *1 ship strength point*. In order to get the sailors, you must bid against the two other traders.

Bidding works like this: You may bid from 10 to 30 gold pieces on any sailor. Note this by writing the number of gold pieces you bid on each sailor in the left-hand column under your name. Then flip the pages twice. Each flip multiplied by 10 represents the bid of one of the other bidders. If you have the highest number or are tied for the highest number, you get the sailor and deduct that number of gold pieces from your *status chart*. Note: You can always win the bid if you are willing to pay the outrageous price of 40 gold pieces per man.

	BIDS		
	Sagard	Hitaxian	Medigian
MAN # 1	_____	_____	_____
MAN # 2	_____	_____	_____
MAN # 3	_____	_____	_____
MAN # 4	_____	_____	_____
MAN # 5	_____	_____	_____
MAN # 6	_____	_____	_____
MAN # 7	_____	_____	_____
MAN # 8	_____	_____	_____
MAN # 9	_____	_____	_____
MAN # 10	_____	_____	_____
MAN # 11	_____	_____	_____
MAN # 12	_____	_____	_____
MAN # 13	_____	_____	_____
MAN # 14	_____	_____	_____
MAN # 15	_____	_____	_____

After the auction, total the number of gold pieces you have spent and deduct them from the amount of gold you have on your *status chart*. Then return to the map (Section 39) and sail far from the Isle of Despair.

Remember, you may not return to any port once you have left it.

3

SECTION 60
The Slaves Find a Home

For several days, your men mingle with the people of the Isle of Hope, and bonds grow. For the first time in memory, you also feel at home. (Regain *all hit points*.) Were it not for the imprisonment of Ketza Kota, you would very possibly stay, but dark imaginings of her fate in the palace of the Sultoon Jazeer raise your hackles, and you resolve to set sail once again.

Setting your men to repairing the ship, return the *Midnight Reaper* to *full ship strength points*. Though neither the islanders nor your men ever want to leave the island, you manage to persuade them to sail with you to Hitaxia where you can rescue your friend. (Gain 5 *experience marks* for finding the slaves a new home.)

Moments before you set sail, Mowanna runs to the ship, bringing you a shield made from the hide of the Sardonus. The *Sardonus shield* can absorb up to 12 damage points in battle before it is destroyed. Note it on your *status chart*.

Return to the map (Section 39) and sail from port on the Isle of Hope. You may not return to this island once you have left it.

SECTION 61
Treacherous Shores

Just off the coast of the Isle of Despair lie some of the most treacherous reefs in the realm. As you sail past the island, coral fingers pointing upward from the depths scratch at the *Midnight Reaper*'s hull like skeletal hands on a tombstone.

As the helmsman desperately tries to avoid the deadly reefs, a hideous crack pierces your ears, and cries of alarm drift up from below decks.

Dashing down to the hold, you see that the bottom of the ship has been ripped open and water is pouring in.

Flip the pages and lose *3 ship strength points* for each number you roll. (For example, if you roll a 2, lose 6 points. If you roll a 3, lose 9 points.) Water continues to flood into the ship! You must get to a port for repairs.

Return to the map (Section 39), point your ship away from the Isle of Despair, and sail for the nearest port. Take 1 damage point for each hex you cross over on the way to port.

SECTION 62
The Pirates Return to Sea

After spending several days resting on the Isle of Hope and repairing your ship (Return your ship to *full ship strength points* and regain *all hit points*), you prepare to sail for the Isle of Dread.

Upon hearing that you intend to sail there, Mowanna's eyes light up. "There is great treasure on the Isle of Dread. It is said to be at the very pinnacle of a mountain and guarded by great eagles who will tear at you with jagged talons. Take this gift, for it might spare your life."

With that, she runs away, only to return moments later with a beautiful *shirt* made from the skin of the Sardonus. This shirt will serve you well, giving you up to 20 *extra hit points* any one time you fight, after which it becomes useless. Mark this on your *status chart*, then move the ship to port on the Isle of Hope (if it is not already there) and set sail.

Remember, you may not return to any island once you have left it.

SECTION 63
The Medigian Trader

The Medigian Trader eyes you with dim recognition. You have seen his gnarled face before but can't remember where.*

Pointing at you, his fingers trembling, he shouts, "Catch that swine! He was a slave of mine who escaped through the treachery of a Valkyrie."

Suddenly, two Medigian sailors attack you. Prepare to defend yourself. They strike first.

SAGARD (LEVEL 3: 1/1, 2/1, 3/2, 4/3)
[20] [19] [18] [17] [16] [15] [14] [13] [12] [11] [10] [9]
[8] [7] [6] [5] [4] [3] [2] [1] **(Begin the book again.)**

MEDIGIAN SAILOR #1 (LEVEL 2: 1/0, 2/1, 3/1, 4/2)
[14] [13] [12] [11] [10] [9] [8] [7] [6] [5] [4] [3] [2] [1]

MEDIGIAN SAILOR #2 (LEVEL 2: 1/0, 2/1, 3/1, 4/2)
[10] [9] [8] [7] [6] [5] [4] [3] [2] [1]

If you defeat your opponents, go to Section 65.

Flee to Section 67.

---

*Sagard the Barbarian Gamebook 1: The Ice Dragon

SECTION 64
King of the Aborites

The Tortoise Man, his shell cracked, falls to the ground. The crowd cheers you. The Tortoise Man was their king. In accordance with their ancient rituals, you are the new king.

For several days, you reign over the Aborites and recover from your battles. (Regain *all hit points.*) One day, the medicine man leads you to a secret cove, where a Hitaxian galleon is hidden.

"Ours!" he grunts. Then, he slashes his dagger in the air to show how they got it from the Hitaxians. This is your chance to sail for Tabu-Bel-Abu.

Training the Aborites to sail takes several days. Many times you very nearly run the ship aground, but in comparatively little time the Aborites are competent sailors.

Return to the map (Section 39) and sail from the place where you reached shore. You must sail directly to Tabu-Bel-Abu. The Hitaxian galleon, a merchant ship, has only 15 ship strength points, not the 30 you had, but it otherwise sails and fights like the *Midnight Reaper*. Note that your crew is composed of Aborites.

SECTION 65
Defeating the Medigian Sailors

Knowing that their end is imminent, the Medigians drop their swords and kneel down. "Spare us, oh great one. Our lives are yours," one of them says, trembling. (Gain *2 experience marks*.)

At the same instant, the Medigian Trader dashes through the crowd, which has gathered to watch the fight.

Seeing men begging at your feet revolts you, but nevertheless you need more crewmen to man your ship.

"I will spare you," you say. "But should you prove mutinous, I will cut you where you stand."

With that, the men on the trading block call to you. "Buy us, Ratikkan, and you shall never be sorry."

At this point, you may buy up to fifteen sailors for 10 gold pieces each. Each sailor will be worth *1 ship strength point*.

After paying the trader (deduct the gold from your *status chart*), you head back to the ship. (Regain *all hit points* once at sea.)

Return to the map (Section 39), and remember that you may not return to any island once you have left it.

SECTION 66
The Sinking of the
Midnight Reaper

(If you have been to this section before, begin the book again. If not, keep reading.)

The last sound you hear is a loud crack, and the last thing you see is water cascading over the side of the *Midnight Reaper*. Then, everything goes black and silent.

Noting the number of this section, return to the map. If you are more than two hexes away from any land mass (whether you have been to it or not), begin the book again. If you can reach a land mass in two hexes, keep reading, If not, you drown and begin the book again.

For a very long time, you swim through the Crimson Sea. Lose all of your treasure and retain only your weapons.

It is night when you awaken on a mysterious shore, more dead than alive. Dragging yourself out of the surf, you collapse on a sandy beach. Days pass on the island shore as breakers slam onto the coast followed by the clatter of colliding rocks. During those days you eat raw fruit and fish, recovering *all hit points*.

One night, you awaken with a start as something tickles your back. Spinning around, you discover

that you are face to face with an enormous eye. The eye is not attached to any head. It comes off of a long stem which is connected to one of the most hideous creatures you have ever seen.

It appears to be a giant lobster. It is nearly seven feet long, and its serrated claws are large enough to snap you in half.

Fire coursing through your veins, you jump to your feet and prepare to flee but are hemmed in by large rocks. If you tried to flee the Giant Lobster, its hideous claws would grab you from behind as you were climbing the rocks and cut you in half. You strike first.

SAGARD (LEVEL 3: 1/1, 2/1, 3/2, 4/3)
[20] [19] [18] [17] [16] [15] [14] [13] [12] [11] [10] [9]
[8] [7] [6] [5] [4] [3] [2] [1] (Begin the book again.)

GIANT LOBSTER (LEVEL 3: 1/1, 2/1, 3/2, 4/3)
[25] [24] [23] [22] [21] [20] [19] [18] [17] [16] [15]
[14] [13] [12] [11] [10] [9] [8] [7] [6] [5] [4] [3] [2] [1]
(When you have defeated the Giant Lobster, go to Section 68.)

You may *not* flee.

SECTION 67
Return to the
Midnight Reaper

A crowd of islanders gathers as you exchange blows with the Medigian sailors. Not wanting to attract further attention, you flee the slave market.

The crowd parts in horror as you race through it. The sailors give chase, but your powerful legs put you far in front of them. Reaching your longboat, you row quickly back to the *Midnight Reaper*.

Regain *15 hit points* and sail away from the port on the Isle of Despair.

You may *not* return to any island once you have visited it.

SECTION 68
Dinner and Armor

Raising your sword high over your head, you deliver an arcing blow to the Giant Lobster. Its shell splits in half, and the hideous creature drops to the sand. (Gain 3 *experience marks*.)

After killing the massive beast, you remove its armored shell and cook the meat underneath. (Regain *13 hit points*.)

While you eat, you eye the armor and get an idea. Removing the hard breast shell from the Giant Lobster, you put it over your chest. It fits perfectly. Using the legs as shin and thigh guards, you have a suit of armor.

The *Giant Lobster armor* shall serve you well. In combat with any opponent, it will knock 2 hit points off every attack from your opponents. Therefore, if an opponent does 3 points of damage to you, it will be reduced to 1, and if he does 2 points of damage to you, it will not count at all.

It is not long before you get a chance to test it out. Burning eyes peer at you from behind jagged rocks, and suddenly arrows arc through the air and stick in your armor but do not penetrate.

As you jump to your feet, four screaming natives come after you. They are Aborites, an island people who paint themselves in garish warpaint much like Frustis and are not known for their hospitality. However, when they see you standing, holding a sword, they break off their attack and begin chanting loudly and dancing around you.

At first you twirl around with them, expecting attack, but as the dance goes on it becomes clear that they think you are part of one of their rituals.

This strange scene goes on for several minutes when other Aborites appear from the center of the island. Building a large fire, the entire tribe joins in the festivities. Singing, clapping, and laughter fill the scene as you wait for a chance to sneak away.

Just as it looks like their attention has shifted away from you, another figure appears. It is a man, armored much the way you are, wearing the shell and leathery skin of a sea tortoise.

Thick claws spring from his hands, and it begins

to dawn on you that you and the Tortoise Man are supposed to join in combat, much like the struggle in nature between giant lobsters and sea tortoises.

You have no choice but to partake in this combat, for were you to flee the entire tribe would overwhelm you.

SAGARD (LEVEL 3: 1/1, 2/1, 3/2, 4/3)
[20] [19] [18] [17] [16] [15] [14] [13] [12] [11] [10] [9] [8] [7] [6] [5] [4] [3] [2] [1] **(Begin the book again.)**

TORTOISE MAN (LEVEL 4: 1/1, 2/2, 3/3, 4/3)
[33] [32] [31] [30] [29] [28] [27] [26] [25] [24] [23] [22] [21] [20] [19] [18] [17] [16] [15] [14] [13] [12] [11] [10] [9] [8] [7] [6] [5] [4] [3] [2] [1] **(When you have defeated your opponent, go to Section 64.)**

You may *not* flee.

SECTION 69
Mutiny Check

If your crew is not composed of pirates, return to the map (Section 39) and keep sailing. If your crew is composed of pirates and you have retrieved the treasure from the Isle of Dread, sail on. If, however, your crew is composed of pirates and you have not retrieved your treasure, keep reading.

As you near the minarets and domes of Hitaxia, a wave of unrest grows among your crew. Standing watch on the deck, you hear sounds behind you. Pirates hover about, cutlasses drawn.

"Aye, Ratikkan, it seems that we are putting in at Hitaxia without the treasure promised us."

You try to persuade them. The only language they understand is gold. You will persuade one sailor for each Hitaxian galleon you have plundered. Thus, if you have plundered no galleons, all four pirates will attack you. If you have plundered one galleon, three of them will attack you. If you have plundered two, two will attack you. If you have plundered three, only one will attack you. And if you have plundered four, you have avoided the mutiny and may sail onward.

SAGARD (LEVEL 3: 1/1, 2/1, 3/2, 4/3)
[20] [19] [18] [17] [16] [15] [14] [13] [12] [11] [10] [9]
[8] [7] [6] [5] [4] [3] [2] [1] (Begin the book again.)

MUTINEERS (LEVEL 2: 1/0, 2/1, 3/1, 4/2)
  MUTINEER #1 [15] [14] [13] [12] [11] [10] [9] [8]
[7] [6] [5] [4] [3] [2] [1]
  MUTINEER #2 [15] [14] [13] [12] [11] [10] [9] [8]
[7] [6] [5] [4] [3] [2] [1]
  MUTINEER #3 [15] [14] [13] [12] [11] [10] [9] [8]
[7] [6] [5] [4] [3] [2] [1]
  MUTINEER #4 [15] [14] [13] [12] [11] [10] [9] [8]
[7] [6] [5] [4] [3] [2] [1]

When you have defeated your opponents, gain
1 experience mark for each one you have defeated, and keep sailing. (Go back to the map after Section 39.)

You may *not* flee the Mutineers.

SECTION 70
A Brace of Hitaxian Warships

(If you have already fought this battle, go to Section 75.)

In this battle, you will fight two Hitaxian cruisers. Remember your three battle options.

Ramming: If you flip a 4, you have sunk the Hitaxian ship. If you flip a 1, it means they are trying to ram you. Flip again. If you flip another 1, you are sunk and go to Section 66.

Missile fire: Both sides fight at the same level (1/0, 2/1, 3/2, 4/3).

Boarding: Count up the number of ship strength points on both sides. Flip for both sides, and deduct one man from the other side each time you flip a 4. After you have flipped for each side, count both sides again and repeat the process until one side is wiped out.

Remember, you only fight one ship at a time. After that, you and the second ship fight. You initiate the combat.

When you sink both of the Hitaxians, gain 5 *experience marks*, return to the map (Section 39), and keep sailing.

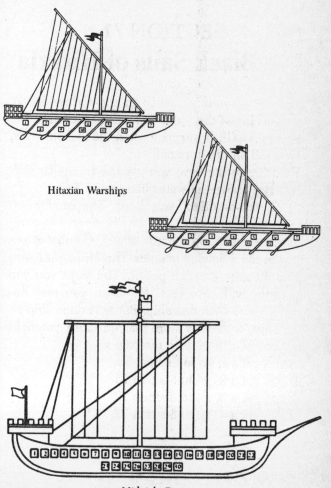

Hitaxian Warships

Midnight Reaper

SECTION 71
The Black Sails of Hitaxia

Warned of your presence in the Crimson Sea, Hitaxians prowl the water in small, fast cruisers.

It comes as little surprise when the lookout cries, "Black sail on the horizon!"

Running to the bow, you spy the triangular sails which rise above the water like sharks' fins.

"All hands on deck!" you shout. "Prepare for battle."

You are about to do battle at sea. Combat at sea works in the following manner. The *Midnight Reaper* has 30 ship strength points. The ships you will encounter will have less. However, you may encounter more than one ship. Battle is done ship by ship. Thus, if there is more than one ship, you fight them one at a time. Flip the pages.

If you get a 1, go to Section 70.

If you get a 2, go to Section 75.

If you get a 3, go to Section 72.

If you get a 4, go to Section 72.

SECTION 72
A Fleet of Warships

(If you have already fought this battle, go to Section 73.)

In this battle, you will fight four Hitaxian cruisers. Remember your three battle options.

Ramming: If you fight a 4, you have sunk the Hitaxian ship. If you flip a 1, flip again. If you flip another 1, you are sunk and go to Section 66.

Missile fire: Both sides fight at the same level (1/0, 2/1, 3/2, 4/3).

Boarding: Count up the number of ship strength points on both sides. Flip for both sides and deduct one man from the other side each time you flip a 4. After you have flipped for each side, count both sides again, and repeat the process until one side is wiped out.

Remember, you only fight one ship at a time. After that, you and the next ship fight. You initiate the type of combat and which ship you fight in each round of combat.

MIDNIGHT REAPER

[30] [29] [28] [27] [26] [25] [24] [23] [22] [21] [20] [19] [18] [17] [16] [15] [14] [13] [12] [11] [10] [9] [8] [7] [6] [5] [4] [3] [2] [1] (If you are sunk, go to Section 66.)

HITAXIAN WARSHIPS

WARSHIP #1 [12] [11] [10] [9] [8] [7] [6] [5] [4] [3] [2] [1]

WARSHIP #2 [12] [11] [10] [9] [8] [7] [6] [5] [4] [3] [2] [1]

WARSHIP #3 [12] [11] [10] [9] [8] [7] [6] [5] [4] [3] [2] [1]

WARSHIP #4 [12] [11] [10] [9] [8] [7] [6] [5] [4] [3] [2] [1]

When you sink all of the Hitaxians, gain 9 *experience marks*, return to the map (Section 39), and keep sailing.

SECTION 73
The Hitaxian Dreadnought

(If you have already fought this battle, return to the map and keep sailing.)

What appeared to be the sail of a small Hitaxian warship turned out to be the mainsail of a massive Hitaxian dreadnought.

Ramming: If you flip a 4, you have sunk the Hitaxian dreadnought. If you flip a 1, you are sunk. Go to Section 66.

Missile fire: Both sides fight at the same level (1/0, 2/1, 3/2, 4/3).

Boarding: Count up the number of ship strength points on both sides. Flip for both sides, and deduct one man from the other side each time you flip a 4. After you have flipped for each side, count both sides again, and repeat the process until one side is wiped out.

Remember, you only fight one ship at a time. After that, you and the second ship fight.

MIDNIGHT REAPER

[30] [29] [28] [27] [26] [25] [24] [23] [22] [21] [20] [19] [18] [17] [16] [15] [14] [13] [12] [11] [10] [9] [8] [7] [6] [5] [4] [3] [2] [1] (If you are sunk, go to Section 66.)

HITAXIAN DREADNOUGHT

[40] [39] [38] [37] [36] [35] [34] [33] [32] [31] [30] [29] [28] [27] [26] [25] [24] [23] [22] [21] [20] [19] [18] [17] [16] [15] [14] [13] [12] [11] [10] [9] [8] [7] [6] [5] [4] [3] [2] [1]

If you sink the dreadnought, gain *10 experience marks* and return to the map (Section 39).

SECTION 74
Pirating a Hitaxian Galleon

(The first time you come to this section, go fight the galleon. Every other time, flip the pages. If you get an even number, fight another galleon.)

Pirating works like this: Before each round of combat, flip the pages. If you get a 4, the Hitaxian galleon surrenders. (Gain *50 gold pieces* for each strength point the Hitaxian ship has.) If you get a 1, flip again. If you get a second 1, the galleon escapes.

If the galleon neither surrenders nor escapes, you must do combat. You may break off the attack and sail away any time you want. Combat works exactly like land combat.

MIDNIGHT REAPER (1/1, 2/1, 3/2, 4/3)
[30] [29] [28] [27] [26] [25] [24] [23] [22] [21] [20]
[19] [18] [17] [16] [15] [14] [13] [12] [11] [10] [9] [8]
[7] [6] [5] [4] [3] [2] [1] (Sunk. Go to Section 66.)

ENCOUNTER 1

HITAXIAN GALLEON (1/0, 2/0, 3/1, 4/1)
[10] [9] [8] [7] [6] [5] [4] [3] [2] [1] (Sunk. Gain no gold pieces.)

ENCOUNTER 2

HITAXIAN GALLEON (1/0, 2/0, 3/1, 4/1)
[10] [9] [8] [7] [6] [5] [4] [3] [2] [1] (Sunk. Gain no
gold pieces.)

ENCOUNTER 3

HITAXIAN GALLEON (1/0, 2/0, 3/1, 4/1)
[10] [9] [8] [7] [6] [5] [4] [3] [2] [1] (Sunk. Gain no
gold pieces.)

ENCOUNTER 4

HITAXIAN GALLEON (1/0, 2/0, 3/1, 4/1)
[10] [9] [8] [7] [6] [5] [4] [3] [2] [1] (Sunk. Gain no
gold pieces.)

If the Hitaxian galleon surrenders, gain *50 gold pieces* for each strength point it has left. If the Hitaxian galleon escapes, you gain nothing.

SECTION 75
A Flotilla of Hitaxian Cruisers

(If you have already fought this battle, go to Section 72.)

In this battle, you will fight three Hitaxian cruisers. Remember your three battle options.

Ramming: If you flip a 4, you have sunk the Hitaxian ship. If you flip a 1, flip again. If you flip another 1, you are sunk and go to Section 66.

Missile fire: Both sides fight at the same level (1/0, 2/1, 3/2, 4/3)

Boarding: Flip once for each strength point you have, and deduct one man from the other side each time you flip a 4. Then do the same for the Hitaxians. After you have flipped for each side, count both sides again. Repeat the process until one side is wiped out or you want to use another battle option.

Remember, you only fight one ship at a time. After that, you and the second ship fight.

MIDNIGHT REAPER
[30] [29] [28] [27] [26] [25] [24] [23] [22] [21] [20] [19] [18] [17] [16] [15] [14] [13] [12] [11] [10] [9] [8] [7] [6] [5] [4] [3] [2] [1] (If you are sunk, go to Section 66.)

HITAXIAN WARSHIPS
    WARSHIP #1 [12] [11] [10] [9] [8] [7] [6] [5] [4] [3] [2] [1]
    WARSHIP #2 [12] [11] [10] [9] [8] [7] [6] [5] [4] [3] [2] [1]
    WARSHIP #3 [12] [11] [10] [9] [8] [7] [6] [5] [4] [3] [2] [1]

When you sink all of the Hitaxians, gain *7 experience marks,* return to the map (Section 39), and keep sailing.

SECTION 76
Attacking the Old Man

Fury coursing in your veins, you raise your sword and deliver a solid blow. However, the sword strikes the ground and, with a mighty clang, snaps in half (Lose your *sword*.)

The old man, who should have been cleaved in half by the blow, smiles up at you.

"Even you, Sagard of Ratik, cannot kill those who are already dead. Now you may understand why I harbor such deep hatred for the Sultoon Jazeer. Also, you might understand why I am able to see those things which are invisible to mortal eyes."

Warily, you back away from the old man, only to step directly into the young boy, who quickly scampers away.

"Beware, Sagard. The girl shall be in grave danger should you attempt to rescue her. Her life shall be long if you do not. Do you still want to attempt to rescue her?" (At this point, you may still forget about your mission against the Sultoon and go to Section 96. If not, keep reading.)

"I will take my chances," you respond.

"Then I shall lead you to the palace tonight. Take my scimitar, for my ghostly hands will be unable to use it."

The old man's *scimitar* is an extremely sharp weapon. Therefore, any time you flip a 4, it will do 5 points of damage. Otherwise, fight at your normal level. Note this on your *status chart*. If you want to carry on with your mission, go to Section 89.

SECTION 77
The High Butte

The wind moans through the buttes like a dying man.

As you climb, two other pirates follow behind you to make sure you are not deceiving them.

High on the mesa, you get a marvelous view of the island. There is not much to see: endless stretches of sand, scratched rock, and mesas.

Reaching the top of the butte, you hear a loud squawk and see a flutter of wings. Two enormous eagles with fifteen-foot wingspans dive on you, their talons poised to rip your flesh.

As they approach, you draw your sword to make a final stand atop the butte. The predators arrive with ear-shattering screams and vanish with the two pirates who had accompanied you.

Clutching your companions in their talons, they fly into the distance. High in the air, they let loose their mighty claws and drop the men to screaming deaths on the rocks below.

Knowing that you would meet the same fate if

you tried to descend from the mesa, you await their second attack.

You will fight each of the birds alternately. The first bird strikes, and you strike it back. Then the second bird strikes, and you strike back.

SAGARD (LEVEL 3: 1/1, 2/1, 3/2, 4/3)
[20] [19] [18] [17] [16] [15] [14] [13] [12] [11] [10] [9] [8] [7] [6] [5] [4] [3] [2] [1] (Begin the book again.)

GIANT EAGLE #1 (LEVEL 2: 1/0, 2/1, 3/1, 4/2)
[12] [11] [10] [9] [8] [7] [6] [5] [4] [3] [2] [1]

GIANT EAGLE #2 (LEVEL 2: 1/0, 2/1, 3/1, 4/2)
[12] [11] [10] [9] [8] [7] [6] [5] [4] [3] [2] [1]

When you have defeated your opponents, go to Section 90.

You may *not* flee.

SECTION 78
Message on the Rock

An old, peg-legged pirate squints as he reads, "Under these rocks are buried the rotted corpses of scurvy mates who attempted to steal my treasure. Gaze upon their bones and shudder." With that, the pirates lift the rock and all can see the contorted, clothed skeletons of several men, their mouths open wide as if they had been screaming when they died.

A hiss of recrimination drifts through the crowd, and the pirates eye you with ill-concealed hatred.

"The Ratikkan dog lied to us about the treasure!" one of the pirates shouts, drawing his cutlass.

Backing up, you draw your sword to take as many with you as you can, but no matter what you do it will be a hideous end.

Begin the book again.

SECTION 79
Revenge of the Dead Kingdom

Fleeing from the palace, you and Ketza Kota climb your thin rope to the dome. In the soft moonlight, you stop to kiss her and then run quickly toward the Davanian bat.

As you are about to take off on the bat, a fiery dagger whizzes past your head. Turning, you see a familiar evil figure silhouetted against the stars. It is tall and thin and clad only in black. Even in the dim light, you are able to see a pair of burning yellow eyes and a long reptilian tongue. It is a Slith Assassin!

"I knew that one day you would come here, Sagard! Tonight I shall avenge the Sliths, and the priestess shall die."

As the Slith Assassin draws a dagger, you kick the bat. It takes off with Ketza Kota. Then, before the Slith Assassin can throw one of his daggers at her, you charge him.

Delivering a desperate blow, you knock the dagger from the Slith Assassin's hand. Stunned, he desperately flees to the top of the dome. You give chase and finally catch him atop the dome. You strike first.

SAGARD (LEVEL 3: 1/1, 2/1, 3/2, 4/3)
[20] [19] [18] [17] [16] [15] [14] [13] [12] [11] [10] [9]
[8] [7] [6] [5] [4] [3] [2] [1] (Begin the book again.)

SLITH ASSASSIN (His fighting level drops with the number of hit points he has.)
(LEVEL 5: 1/2, 2/3, 3/3, 4/4)
[25] [24] [23] [22] [21] [20]
(LEVEL 4: 1/1, 2/2, 3/3, 4/3)
[19] [18] [17] [16] [15] [14]
(LEVEL 3: 1/1, 2/1, 3/2, 4/3)
[13] [12] [11] [10] [9]
(LEVEL 2: 1/0, 2/1, 3/1, 4/2)
[8] [7] [6] [5]
(LEVEL 1: 1/0, 2/0, 3/1, 4/1)
[4] [3] [2] [1] (When you have defeated him, go to Section 87.)

If you flee, go to Section 81.

SECTION 80
The Mysterious Island

Anchoring your ship in a small bay, you observe the barren and desolate island. Neither man nor plant nor animal appears to live on this wind-scarred dot of mesas and blowing sands. (Gain *1 experience mark* for successfully landing.)

If you wish to do repairs, flip the pages and multiply the number you get by 5. Then return that many ship strength points to your ship.

If your crew is made up of slaves, go back to the map (Section 39) and set sail again.

If your crew is made up of pirates, keep reading.

A hot, dry wind blows up from the south, making the pirates' short tempers even shorter. As you step onto the island, you feel a menacing, foreboding presence.

The island looks haunted. A ghost forest of fossilized trees resembles a graveyard, and tall buttes, sculpted by the hot winds into bizarre shapes, loom over you like stone phantoms.

Low rumblings of mutiny are heard from pirates' mouths as you begin the quest.

There are three promising places to search for treasure on the island. Near the center of the island are a number of piled boulders (Section 86). To the south is a chimney-shaped mesa which stands taller than any of the others (Section 77), and to the north is a steep butte with dozens of mysterious holes in the side of it (Section 92).

SECTION 81
Fleeing the Slith Assassin

As the Slith Assassin pulls a fresh dagger from his vest, you jump out of the way. You lose your balance and slide helplessly down the side of the dome, landing on the hard stone. Take 2 hit points of damage. If you still survive, keep reading.

You watch in helpless horror as the Slith Assassin pulls a fire dart from his vest and throws it. The hideous projectile streaks across the sky after the bat and Ketza Kota.

When it hits, there is a burst of light and then . . . nothing.

Picking yourself up off the ground, you notice for the first time that chaos has overtaken the palace. Men of all descriptions battle each other for the Sultoon's throne before his body is cold. Such are the politics of Hitaxia.

Thus, in the chaos, you are largely unnoticed as you slip through the gate and head into the city, which is ablaze with activity.

Hours later, you arrive in the bazaar. As earlier, the ghost plays a hand with his cards. "I warned you of what might become of the girl," the ghost says. "But perhaps you shall meet again in another life."

Your hand flashes to the hilt of your sword, but you quickly draw it away. You have no recourse against a ghost.

"I would extend my sympathies," the ghost says. "But death isn't really that bad . . . just a little tedious at times." Looking up at you, he points to a tattered box across the room. "Take something from my chest of treasure."

Stepping to the chest, you break the lock with your sword. Inside is an unbelievable trove of treasure which gleams even in the flickering candlelight!

Picking up the chest, you walk to the door. The ghost reacts in horror. "Take some of it, but do not be greedy," he calls.

Ignoring his shouts, you step to the door. The ghost chases you; however, his attempts to grab you are futile. Gain 2,000 gold pieces and 1 experience mark, and go to Section 96.

2

SECTION 82
Marooned on the Isle of Dread

Badly wounded by the hideous flying serpents, you crawl out of their short flying range. With the two other survivors, you crawl back toward the ship.

Time and venom have taken away your strength, and after several hours of desperate crawling you collapse beneath a brittle fossil tree.

Eyeing the barren white mesas, you know what your bones will soon look like.

Begin the book again.

SECTION 83
Defeating the Genie

The Genie, badly hurt and outraged, raises his sword and charges you. Dodging away, you bump into the Sultoon, which sends the Sultoon's lamp flying. The Sultoon hurls himself toward the lamp and into the Genie's path.

Seeing this, the Sultoon shouts, "Stop!" The Genie tries to obey but lands squarely on the Sultoon, crushing him *and* the lamp. (Gain 6 *experience marks*.)

You grab Ketza Kota and begin climbing the rope out of the banquet hall. The Genie, seeing what he has done, shrieks in insane fury as the Sultoon's guards arrive. Chaos breaks loose, giving you and Ketza Kota time to escape. Go to Section 79.

SECTION 84
The Isle of Gold

As you draw near the Isle of Gold, a rock cracks into the side of the ship.

Peering over the side, you see that the coastline teems with floating rocks.

You alert the pilot, and he tries to swing the ship away. You suddenly hear another loud crack and see a massive boulder just off the port bow.

As the day goes on, several of these boulders thud against the ship, but you miraculously escape damage. However, with the afternoon come dark clouds. The placid ocean suddenly turns turbulent.

Flip the pages. If you get an even number, go to

Section 66. If you get an odd number, keep reading.

In the storm, several boulders crack against the hull, and the helmsman shouts that the *Midnight Reaper* is taking in water.

You must get to a port fast. Take 1 point of ship damage for each hex you sail through on the way to any port you haven't been to before.

SECTION 85
Stealing the Lamp

As the Genie reels about in confusion from your last attack, you rush the Sultoon Jazeer. The Sultoon, fearing your unspent fury, quickly jumps from his seat and drops the lamp.

Grabbing the lamp, you see the Genie poised to destroy you. However, when he realizes that you hold the lamp, he bows. "Grab the Sultoon and tear the palace to the ground," you shout. (Gain 3 *experience marks*.)

The Genie then chases after the fleeing man. Meanwhile, hearing the rhythmic footsteps of the palace guard, you take Ketza Kota by the hand, dash to the rope, and begin climbing.

Down below, the Genie grabs the Sultoon Jazeer and throws him overhand through another great window, arcing over the skyline of Tabu-Bel-Abu.

Reaching the top of the dome, you and Ketza Kota climb up. Arrows fly through the window after you as the Genie desperately battles the palace guards. Go to Section 79.

SECTION 86
Moving the Boulders

Upon reaching the boulders, you order your men to move the massive stones.

As they do, you wait nervously.

Finally, the job is complete, and under the boulders is a stone with a strange foreign message carved on it.

One of the sailors, fluent in the language, reads it and looks up at you.

You sweat profusely. If there is no treasure under the rock, the pirates will mutiny.

If you told the pirates that you knew where the treasure was, go to Section 78. If the pirates learned about the treasure through rumors, go to Section 88.

SECTION 87
Defeating the Slith Assassin

Jabbing upward, you hit the Slith Assassin. He stumbles for a moment, then tumbles like a rag doll down the side of the dome. Steeling the last of your strength, you step to the window, only to see the Genie's lifeless body on the floor, surrounded by Hitaxian guards. (Gain 3 *experience marks*.)

Knowing that you have little time left, you slide down the dome. When you reach the ground, you discover that the palace is in chaos. People run in all directions. Taking advantage of the chaos, you dash to the gate and flee.

Hours later, you arrive in the bazaar. Once again, the ghost is reading his tarot cards.

"Where is she?" you demand. "Where did you have the bat take her?"

"She is far away," the ghost responds. "Where you were supposed to be. I did not think you would be so successful."

"Where is she?" you demand, not accepting his last answer.

"That is not for me to tell, for the cards say you will not see her again for several years. And then it will be by chance."

Angered, you instinctively grip the hilt of your sword, but you quickly draw your hand away. You have no recourse against a ghost.

"However," the old man says, "I owe you quite a bit. Take what you want from my chest of treasure."

He points to a tattered chest across the room. Whacking it with your sword, you break the lock. Even in the flickering candlelight of the stall, the treasure gleams!

Picking up the chest, you walk to the door. The ghost reacts in horror. "Take some of it, but do not be greedy," he calls.

But you ignore his shouts and step to the door. The angry ghost gets up and chases you; however, his attempts to grab you are as futile as your attempt to whack him with your sword. Gain *2,000 gold pieces* and go to Section 96.

SECTION 88
Beneath the Rock

The old, gnarled Fexian pirate squints as he reads, "Under these rocks are buried the bones of scurvy mates who attempted to steal my treasure. Gaze upon their horror and shudder." With that, the pirates lift the rock and see the contorted clothed skeletons of several men, their mouths open wide as if they had been screaming when they died.

A hiss of recrimination drifts through the crowd, and fights break out. Four men die before you can quell the quarrel. (Lose *4 ship strength points*.)

"As you were, men. We must search in at least one more place."

With a low, discontented rumble, the men calm down. Now you may lead them to one of the other search points. To climb the tall mesa and inspect the island, go to Section 77. To investigate the steep butte, go to Section 92.

SECTION 89
The Sultoon Jazeer's Palace

You and the old man creep silently under the light of the Hitaxian moon.

Before setting out, the ghost made you promise to help him gain revenge against the Sultoon before freeing Ketza Kota. Though you argued, you soon realized that you had little hope of success without him.

Climbing to the top of a small hill, the ghost points out the Sultoon's palace. Surrounded by high outer battlements and ringed with tall minarets is a huge dome. At the top of the walls and each minaret are Hitaxian archers wearing tall, pointed caps.

"The Sultoon Jazeer, as befits his conceit, lives at the top of the great dome, protected by guards everywhere. As you see, Sagard," the ghost mutters to you, "there is no way in from the ground. You would be pincushioned by arrows, for the Sultoon employs the best archers in the realm."

"If there is no way in, then how am I to succeed?"

With that, the ghost lets out a loud whistle and smiles gleefully. "From above." In moments, a fluttering black shape appears on the horizon and wings its way to the hill where you stand.

As it draws closer, you shudder, for it looks like something only a demon or demented sorcerer could create. In all ways it is like a bat, save for its wingspan, which is nearly ten feet across. The young boy you met in the street rides it atop a high saddle.

"From whence did this horror come?" you ask.

"It is a Davanian bat. Quite common among the Slate Mountains. The Davanians use them in place of horses—and so shall you."

You shudder as you approach the creature, but despite its ugly appearance it seems friendly. As you get on top of it, the ghost explains how it is ridden.

The bat carries you into the star-studded night sky of Hitaxia. In moments you reach the outer battlements of the Sultoon's palace and drift over them.

Up close, the palace is breathtakingly beautiful, built in grandiose proportions and composed of diaphanous milky-white marble of unreal purity. Surrounded by minarets, the bulbous dome crowns the entire palace like a halo.

Pulling on the bat's reins, you descend to the great dome. Suddenly, you hear a shout from one of the minarets, followed by the twang of a powerful bow.

The arrows streak toward you. Flip the pages six times and take 2 hit points each time you flip a 4 (no matter what kind of armor you are wearing).

Nearing the dome, you hear the jarring clang of alarm bells from high on the minarets and see men scrambling about the courtyard.

Landing on the dome, you hitch the bat to the carved stonework and creep to the top of the great ball of marble, where you find a window and peer inside.

Far below, in the Sultoon's throne room, a banquet is in progress. Seated at a great table, kept cool by fan bearers, and surrounded by various brightly dressed Hitaxian princes, emirs, and satraps is a small, fat man with wine running down his face.

Without doubt, this is the Sultoon Jazeer. Your anger peaks when you discover that seated next to him is Ketza Kota, dressed in the sparse costume of a dancing girl.

Your sword powered by anger, you smash the window, and brightly colored glass showers down on the dining table, causing the guests to flee for the door.

"How dare you leave me without my permission!" the Sultoon shouts to his fleeing guests, "I will have your cowardly heads for it."

"You won't be alive long enough to have my head," one guest responds to the fat despot.

In the confusion, you drop the rope and shinny down until you are low enough to drop to the table.

Upon seeing you, Ketza Kota shouts, "Sagard!" As you land on the table, you draw your sword and prepare to make good your pledge to the ghost.

The Sultoon, much to your surprise, barely moves. He lifts a small oil lamp with chubby fingers and gives you an oily smile. "Did you think it would be so easy to steal my favorite harem girl and slay me, Ratikkan?"

"Who is going to stop me?" you shout, stepping toward him.

Unperturbed, the Sultoon rubs his ruby-laden hand against the lamp, and a thick green smoke rises in a great pillar. When the smoke clears, there stands a tall, turbaned Genie!

"Destroy him," shouts the Sultoon, laughing and sitting back confident of the outcome. The Genie, pulling a scimitar that is nearly your height from his belt, steps over to attack you. You must fight the Genie, but knowing that you have little chance of defeating him, you try to connive a way to grab the lamp from the Sultoon and thus turn the Genie on the Sultoon.

Stealing the lamp works in the following manner: Fight as you would normally. However, each time you flip a 4, you have stunned the Genie and may therefore try to get the lamp by flipping another 4. If you have a *stun stone,* you may also use it, and each time you successfully stun the Genie you may try to get the lamp.

SAGARD (LEVEL 3: 1/1, 2/1, 3/2, 4/3)
[20] [19] [18] [17] [16] [15] [14] [13] [12] [11] [10] [9] [8] [7] [6] [5] [4] [3] [2] [1] **(Begin the book again.)**

GENIE (LEVEL 5: 1/2, 2/3, 3/3, 4/4)
[40] [39] [38] [37] [36] [35] [34] [33] [32] [31] [30] [29] [28] [27] [26] [25] [24] [23] [22] [21] [20] [19][18] [17] [16] [15] [14] [13] [12] [11] [10] [9] [8] [7] [6] [5] [4] [3] [2] [1] **(Go to Section 83.)**

If you steal the lamp, go to Section 85.

You may *not* flee.

SECTION 90
Mesa of the Giant Eagles

The second Giant Eagle, its wing ripped from its body, crashes to the ground with a hideous scream. (Gain 2 *experience marks*.) Far below, your men cheer, and you proudly raise your sword. Suddenly, the mesa beneath you crumbles, dropping you a yard down.

As you struggle to get out of the newly formed hole, you hear soft metallic clicks. Looking down, you discover that you are up to your knees in treasure!

Marveling at the genius of the pirate who buried his treasure above the ground, you shower your men with plunder. (Gain *1,500 gold pieces*.)

At the bottom of the chest, below the gold, jewels, and pearls, is an ornate iron *breastplate* and *shin greaves* that must have been made for a king. There is no question in your mind, or in the minds of your men, who will get this treasure.

The king's *breastplate* and *shin greaves* will make you nearly invulnerable to low-level attackers. As long as you wear them, they will deduct 2 hit points from any attack on you, and if you are ever in need of money, the armor will sell for 1,000 gold pieces. Note it on your *status chart*.

For two days, the men revel on the Isle of Dread, and you regain *all of your hit points*. Return to the map (Section 39), much richer, and sail away.

SECTION 91
Making an Ally

"I saw the fire in your eyes, lad, and you did well to douse it." The old man rises, and you are horrified to discover that you can see all the way through him. "For even you, Sagard, cannot kill those who are already dead. The Sultoon Jazeer killed me. In life I was sultoon, but now I am a ghost. For holding in your anger, I shall give you the stun stone."

The old man gestures to the young boy, who

scampers off and fetches a box. When he opens the box, a painful, blinding light strikes you, and you are temporarily paralyzed.

In the box is the *stun stone*. If used properly, it will help you in difficult combat. Any time you show it, it will give you 2 free attacks. However, you *must* use it sparingly. Each time you wish to use it, flip the pages. If you flip a 4, flip again. If you flip a 3 or a 4 the second time, it has shattered and you may not use it again. Note this on your *status chart*.

"Beward, Sagard. The girl shall be in grave danger should you attempt to rescue her. Her life shall be long if you do not. Do you still want to attempt to rescue her?" (At this point, you may still forget about your mission against the Sultoon and go to Section 96. If not, keep reading.)

"I will take my chances," you respond.

"Then I shall lead you to the palace tonight."

Go to Section 89.

SECTION 92
The Butte with 1,000 Holes

The pirate's treasure could be in any of the pocked holes which seem to watch over the isle like the eyes of a skull. Approaching the butte cautiously, you order your men to search in pairs.

Entering a dark, dry cave, you brush away a curtain of cobwebs. Your ears are first tickled by the sound of fluttering wings, then by the hiss of serpents. Warily, you watch the ground.

A few feet away, you hear a blood-curdling scream and see the pirate who accompanied you desperately grasping the body of a winged serpent that is coiled around his neck.

With a deft whack, you slice the serpent's body in half. Instead of dying, the reptile attacks you with dripping fangs!

Delivering a precise blow, you destroy the serpent in midair, but there is no moment of celebration, for several more wing toward you.

As you struggle to save your companion, you hear screams from the other caves. The same terror strikes them as well.

As you flee the caves, flip the pages for each ship strength point you have and deduct one crewman for each 4 you flip.

If you have less than 5 ship strength points left, go to Section 82. If you have 5 or more ship strength points, go to Section 94.

SECTION 93
Horror from the Depths

Many omens foretell the coming of the great horror. The seas are calm—perhaps too calm. The graceful seagulls that follow in your wake have vanished, and the red seaweed from which the Crimson Sea has gotten its name is particularly thick, making the ocean look like an unbounded pool of blood.

Still, nothing but the peculiar legends placed on ancient maps has prepared you for the horror you are about to face.

Without warning, eight massive tentacles, as thick as great redwood trees and covered with suction cups, pierce the ocean surface and wrap themselves around your ship.

As the hull begins to crack, a hideous head with two eyes as black as death rises from the water and begins to gnaw at the prow. Spinning around, you narrowly avoid the grasp of a slimy tentacle, which grabs a running sailor and carries him, screaming, under the ocean.

Most of your men are hardened by the brutal realities of the sea, but they panic and most flee below decks. Gripping your sword, however, you with but a handful of men prepare to do battle with this octopuslike horror, this horror from the depths.

You must fight the Serpent to the death. To destroy it, you must sever each of the tentacles. Though in most combat you may not divide damage among different opponents, you may do so against the Serpent. Therefore, if you flip a 4, doing 5 points of damage, you may use 3 of the points to polish off one tentacle and allocate the other 2 to the next tentacle.

In each round of combat, flip for each tentacle. When you have destroyed a tentacle, it may not fight anymore. The Serpent strikes first.

MIDNIGHT REAPER (1/2, 2/3, 3/4, 4/5)
[30] [29] [28] [27] [26] [25] [24] [23] [22] [21] [20]
[19] [18] [17] [16] [15] [14] [13] [12] [11] [10] [9] [8]
[7] [6] [5] [4] [3] [2] [1] (Sunk. Go to Section 66.)

THE SERPENT (1/0, 2/0, 3/1, 4/1)
   TENTACLE #1 [5] [4] [3] [2] [1]
   TENTACLE #2 [5] [4] [3] [2] [1]
   TENTACLE #3 [5] [4] [3] [2] [1]
   TENTACLE #4 [5] [4] [3] [2] [1]
   TENTACLE #5 [5] [4] [3] [2] [1]
   TENTACLE #6 [5] [4] [3] [2] [1]
   TENTACLE #7 [5] [4] [3] [2] [1]
   TENTACLE #8 [5] [4] [3] [2] [1]

If you defeat the Serpent, gain *6 experience marks,* and return to the map (Section 39). If you are badly damaged, sail to a port for repairs.

You may *not* flee.

SECTION 94
Flight from the Flying Serpents

Regrouping after the vicious attack of the flying serpents, you must search again for the treasure. Knowing that no pirate, no matter how intent on hiding his gold, would have hidden it in the caves, you have a choice of searching either among the boulders (Section 86) or on top of the mesa (Section 77).

SECTION 95
Tabu-Bel-Abu

The sun hangs high in a pure blue sky as the *Midnight Reaper* comes within sight of Tabu-Bel-Abu. At first, the great city appears as a thin white line on the Hitaxian coast, but drawing closer you make out individual domes, towers, minarets, and pointed spires.

By late afternoon, the ship comes near port. A mass of people of all races, from proud kings of the Momboddo Empire to white-haired Vulzar barbarians, swarm about the docks like insects. Never before have you seen battlements as tall or as sturdy as those that surround this city.

Close to shore, you order a longboat dropped and say farewell to your traveling companions, for you have reached your destination and they still have long voyages to make.

A blistering midafternoon heat rises off the dockside streets as you push your way through the clamor of the crowd.

Adjacent to the dock is the bazaar. Here, merchants dressed like sultoons from childhood tales call to you, inviting you to spend money in their stalls, which sell everything from grotesque animals to delicate pastries.

It is not long before a young boy dressed in bright garb and wearing a pair of pointed shoes with bells attached to the ends approaches you. You stifle a laugh at his ridiculous garb as he speaks to you through a long, drooping mustache, which is obviously fake. "You look to be lost, Ratikkan. I show you the city,"

For several moments, you haggle over a price, and he invites you to come out of the sun and into his stall.

With the rattle of beads, you are led into the stall. Once inside, you discover a small ornate room. Carpets have been fastened to the walls, and a strange brass candelabra hangs from the ceiling. It stinks of foreign scents which burn in a small bowl.

For a moment, you feel as though you are about to be overwhelmed by the fumes. Lunging at the bowl, you hurl it out of the room and onto the street.

Your guide turns around in alarm. "What have you done?"

"I will not be fooled so easily. You intended to bring me in here and drug me with that foul stench."

"Oh no, my friend, that is incense of sandalwood, musk, and myrrh," he responds, showing you more incense.

With that, loud laughter erupts on the far side of

the room, and you see a strange figure sitting in the corner. Your flesh tingles, for the old man, who wears a flowing silk gown, was not in the room when you entered, and you did not see him arrive.

As the young boy runs to recover his bowl, the old man motions for you to sit down. Grasping the hilt of your sword, you remain standing.

"Very well, then, stand if you must," he says. With long, bony fingers, the old man reaches for a deck of cards, which are emblazoned with strange drawings. Chanting slightly under his breath, he lays them out in an odd order.

After laying out the cards, the old man looks up at you. Beneath a mane of white hair glow shimmering blue eyes, which seem to sparkle with a much younger age than his own. "The cards told me you would come, and now they tell me what you will do here."

"I do not believe in foul southern magic," you say, turning to leave.

"You have come from the north to rescue a Slith maiden from the palace of the Sultoon Jazeer."

"How could you know that?" you ask, drawing your sword.

"In the cards, I see much more," he says. "I see tears of joy but also tears of grief should you succeed."

At this point, you have a choice. You may end your quest here and tally up your treasure and weapons (Section 96), or you may continue with your mission. If you want to continue, keep reading.

"Nothing shall stop my quest!" you say.

"Very well," he responds. "But do not say I did not warn you."

You boldly step toward the man, your sword drawn. "If I let you live, you might warn the Sultoon of me."

"And if you strike me you will have lost a valuable ally. For I hate the Sultoon more than you do," he responds.

You must make a choice. Either attack the old man (Section 76), or make him into an ally (Section 91).

SECTION 96
Tales in the Hot Wind

A hot desert wind brings strange tales to the city of minarets and dark sorcery. Deep in the casbah, where swarthy-faced, turbaned men smoke from long pipes and tell tales of fantastic treasures, a man all in black with a garish golden earring beckons you. "Come, Ratikkan, for I read your mind."

You turn to see his beady brown eyes staring deeply into yours. "Forget the small plunders you seek here, for there is a much greater treasure in the deep jungles, waiting for you if you have the strength to wrest it from evil hands."

"I have heard of no such treasure," you say.

He waves his hand for you to sit. "Then stay for a moment, and I shall tell you of the Lost City of Ivory."

Make a note of the *experience marks*, the *treasure*, and the *weapons* and *armor* you have gained in this book, for they will help you as you search for the Lost City of Ivory in Book 4 . . .

THE FIRE DEMON

SECTION 97
Fighting Rules

Instructions always make things seem more complicated than they really are. If you have made it this far in the book, the fighting rules should be a snap. Basically, they are common sense. When in doubt about anything, consider what would happen in a real-life situation.

BEFORE PLAYING

All you really need to play this game are this book and a pencil. Some players find that a four-sided die will make fighting quicker, but the random numbers printed on the upper corners of the right-hand pages will generate the combat results perfectly well.

If you have gotten to this page, you know the basics of moving from one section to another. Now, all that is left to learn is how to fight and how to use the Sagard *status sheet* and *status chart*.

FIGHTING

In a number of places in this book, you will encounter enemies and choose to, or *have* to, fight them. There can only be three possible outcomes to a fight: you can *win, lose,* or *flee.*

Winning a fight: You win a fight when you have reduced an enemy's hit points to zero. Or, in situations when you are fighting more than one enemy, you win when you have reduced all of the enemies' hit points to zero.

Losing a fight: You lose a fight when your number of available hit points falls to zero.

Fleeing a fight: When you feel that you might lose a particular fight, or that the fight isn't worth having, you may try to flee. Fleeing is a 50–50 proposition. If you flip the pages and get an even number, you have successfully fled.

You may only attempt to flee before your combat turn, and only once per round.

When you have successfully fled, look in the "flee" section of the combat page, and it will direct you to another page.

Be warned: Some adversaries are impossible to flee from. They are specially marked. If you fail to flee, continue the combat normally.

3

HOW COMBAT WORKS

Combat takes place in rounds and is resolved by generating random numbers from 1 to 4. The tool for doing this is included in the book. Note that there is a number from 1 to 4 printed on the upper corner of each page. If you look away and flip randomly through the book, stopping before you get to the end, you will have a random number.

To have combat, Sagard and his opponent (or opponents) take turns. Unless otherwise stated, Sagard strikes first. After he strikes, the opponent strikes. That completes one round of combat. Combat can go into several rounds and must end when Sagard wins, loses, or flees. When this happens, follow the instructions on that page. These will direct you to your next adventure.

Every battle you fight will be different. The difficulty of each battle will be determined by how many hit points your opponent has and what your opponent's fighting level is.

Hit points are the number of points of damage a player may take before being out of the combat. As Sagard, you are given 20 hit points in the beginning of the game. (This number will change in the course of the game, though in this book Sagard may not exceed 20 hit points.) That means you will have to take 20 points of damage before you are out of the game.

A typical battle sheet looks like this:

SAGARD (LEVEL 3: 1/1, 2/1, 3/2, 4/3)
[20] [19] [18] [17] [16] [15] [14] [13] [12] [11] [10] [9]
[8] [7] [6] [5] [4] [3] [2] [1] (You may fight no more.
Hobble to Section X.)

Each time you score a hit or hits on an opponent, cross out the total number of boxes' worth of damage you do on the opponent's chart, like so:

ORC (LEVEL 1: 1/0, 2/0, 3/1, 4/1)
[12] [11] [10] [9] [8] [7] [6] [5] [4] [3] [2] [1] (You
have successfully defeated the Orc. Go to Section
X.)

As illustrated above, different characters have different *combat levels*. Sagard begins as a Level 3 fighter. Combat levels go from 0 to 5. The higher the combat level, the more dangerous the opponent is. The important fighting information is included in every melee so that you don't need to refer to the chart presented here except when you increase a level.

FIGHTING LEVEL TABLE
Flip Die Roll

	1	2	3	4
Level 0	0	0	0	1
Level 1	0	0	1	1
Level 2	0	1	1	2
Level 3	1	1	2	3
Level 4	1	2	3	3
Level 5	2	3	3	4

These numbers refer to hit points, or damage points. For instance, if Sagard, a Level 3 fighter, gets a 4, he does 3 hit points of damage to his opponent and crosses them off the enemy's chart. Likewise, if a Level 5 fighter gets a 1, he does 2 points of damage. Just to test yourself, what happens if a Level 3 fighter gets a 2?

If you said 1 point of damage, you are correct.

Therefore, the dangerousness of an opponent can be determined by looking at both the fighting level and the number of hit points the opponent has.

Remember, there can only be three possible outcomes to any fight: win, lose, or flee. If your number drops to zero, read the section after the hit points and follow those instructions. Hit points are permanent, but Sagard will frequently rest or eat and regain points. Regained points will be clearly stated in the book.

Bear in mind that the number of Sagard's hit points will go up and down in the course of the game. Sagard carries damage from battle to battle. After each battle, mark Sagard's available hit points on the Sagard *status sheet* (see opposite). Do likewise when Sagard regains hit points.

CURRENT STATUS SHEET
Conflict

	1	2	3	4	5	6	7	8	9	10
	20	20	20	20	20	20	20	20	20	20
S	19	19	19	19	19	19	19	19	19	19
A	18	18	18	18	18	18	18	18	18	18
G	17	17	17	17	17	17	17	17	17	17
A	16	16	16	16	16	16	16	16	16	16
R	15	15	15	15	15	15	15	15	15	15
D'	14	14	14	14	14	14	14	14	14	14
S	13	13	13	13	13	13	13	13	13	13
	12	12	12	12	12	12	12	12	12	12
H	11	11	11	11	11	11	11	11	11	11
I	10	10	10	10	10	10	10	10	10	10
T	9	9	9	9	9	9	9	9	9	9
	8	8	8	8	8	8	8	8	8	8
P	7	7	7	7	7	7	7	7	7	7
O	6	6	6	6	6	6	6	6	6	6
I	5	5	5	5	5	5	5	5	5	5
N	4	4	4	4	4	4	4	4	4	4
T	3	3	3	3	3	3	3	3	3	3
S	2	2	2	2	2	2	2	2	2	2
	1	1	1	1	1	1	1	1	1	1
	0	0	0	0	0	0	0	0	0	0

BONUSES

Along the way, you will pick up bonuses for your journey. These come in three forms: experience marks, weapons and armor, and special items. Each of these bonuses is valuable to you in a different way.

Experience marks are permanent. Sagard will take them with him from book to book. The purpose of experience marks is to determine Sagard's combat level. At the beginning of this book, Sagard is at Level 3. However, once his experience marks total 60, he immediately moves up to Level 4.

Weapons and armor are valuable for combat and will give Sagard an edge when fighting. The value of these weapons will be explained when the weapon is awarded.

Special items serve their own purposes. Some special items, such as shields, can be used to absorb hit points. Others, such as magic potions, can be used to restore hit points when Sagard needs them.

Bonuses and combat results are recorded on the Sagard *status chart* opposite.

SAGARD STATUS CHART

Experience Marks   **Level** **Gold**

Current Hit Points   **Ship Strength Points**

                             _____

                             _____

Weapons and Armor   **Effect on Combat**

_____   _____

_____   _____

_____   _____

_____   _____

_____

Special Items   **Powers**

_____   _____

_____   _____

_____   _____

_____   _____

_____   _____

Ship's Crew Status_____

Each time Sagard is involved in combat or regains hit points, update this *status sheet*. Sagard starts out with 20 hit points. Suppose he loses 8 of them—he is left with 12. Then, let us say he eats and regains 5 hit points in the next section; therefore, he now has 17 hit points. Next time you go into battle, remember how many hit points you have and modify your *status sheet* accordingly. Remember, Sagard may never have more than 20 hit points.

ABOUT THE AUTHORS

GARY GYGAX is the co-creator of the DUNGEONS & DRAGONS® Game, the wildly popular fantasy role-playing game. He is the Chairman of the Board and president of TSR, Inc., the company that produces it.

FLINT DILLE was part of George Lucas's development team for the "Star Wars" TV show. He has written scripts for various animated television series in the U.S.A., including "G.I. Joe," "Mr. T," "Robo-Force," and "Transformers." Most recently, Mr. Dille story-edited the script for the *Transformers* movie.

ABOUT THE ILLUSTRATOR

LESLIE MORRILL is an award-winning children's book illustrator in the U.S.A.

SAGARD
THE BARBARIAN

A new solo adventure series from the legendary co-creator of the Dungeons and Dragons™ game

Enter the realm of Sagard – heroic warrior of the barbarian world – to challenge the seen and unseen forces of evil. You, the reader, became Sagard, and *only you* can fight the battles, make the choices and take the chances at each turn of the page.

There can be no going back – no surrender!

SAGARD THE BARBARIAN: No 1: THE ICE DRAGON

You are Sagard – a young Barbarian – battling the terrors of the Northern Wilderness. In accordance with an age-old tribal custom, you must face the Ordeal of Courage to become a fully-fledged warrior! You will encounter the deadliest of enemies: the razor-clawed Devil Bear and the hideous Great Furred Serpent. But the supreme test of your courage will be to survive the lair of the Ice Dragon!

SBN 0 552 52318 6

SAGARD THE BARBARIAN: No 2: THE GREEN HYRDA

As the lone survivor of a bloody ambush, you – as Sagard – must carry out a life-or-death mission for your homeland and tribe. You will encounter unimaginable horrors in this quest: the indestructible Smoke Demon, the hideous Nightripper and the Slith Assassin. But will you survive the most dangerous adventure of your life in the Tomb of the Green Dragon?

SBN 0 552 52319 4

SAGARD THE BARBARIAN: No 4: THE FIRE DEMON

You are Sagard – the Barbarian – battling your way through the heart of the jungle in search of the lost city of Sanda Uul that has fallen into the clutches of a demonic sorcerer. You will encounter the hideous slithering Slimer, bloodthirsty assassins and greyfleshed, soul-less zombies but will you fall victim of The Curse of Ushad and be engulfed by the flames of The Fire Demon?

SBN 0 552 52343 7

DRAGON WARRIORS

THE ULTIMATE ROLE-PLAYING GAME

DRAGON WARRIORS is the key to a magic world. A land of cobwebbed forests and haunted castles. A land where dire monsters lurk in the shadows of the night, where hobgoblins shriek across the bleak and misty moors, where wizards and armoured warriors roam dank dungeons in their questr for gold and glory. The realm of your imagination.

In DRAGON WARRIORS *you and your friends* become the mighty heroes of fantasy. Ten minutes is all it takes to commence battle with your first foe! Only your own skill and daring, and the decisions you make will stand between you and a hundred hideous deaths!

BOOK ONE: DRAGON WARRIORS
by Dave Morris

This first book gives you the essential rules for you and your friends to enter this world; maps, encounter charts, a rich collection of bloodthirsty monsters, tactical guides and a complete scenario for your first adventure.

SBN 0 552 52287 2

BOOK TWO: THE WAY OF WIZARDRY
by Dave Morris

The second book expands the game to include the magical arts. Take on the mantle of a Mystic or a spell-casting Sorcerer: more than a hundred spells, potions and arcane magical devices await within for you and your friends, together with two eerie scenarios to test your nerve and magical skills!

SBN 0 552 52288 0

BOOK THREE: THE ELVEN CRYSTALS
by Oliver Johnson

Based on the rules and systems detailed in Books One and Two of the series, this third book presents linked scenarios to take you and your friends to the limits of your skill and endurance, together with new monsters, magic and treasure to extend the basic rules of the series.

SBN 0 552 52289 9

BOOK FOUR: OUT OF THE SHADOWS
by Dave Morris

Out of the shadows stalk night's black agents – the Assassins. Book Four presents the full rules for Assassins – techniques of stealth and the martial arts as well as arcane alchemy, mysterious trance-magic and the unstoppable power of the *Death Vow*, together with three enthralling scenarios using these new dark skills!

SBN 0 552 52333 X